HAIRY SITUATIONS

Crisis Planning, Response and Recovery for Your Pet Business

Sonya Wilson

The information and advice presented in this book are based on the author's study and experience. This book is meant to be a guideline for crisis preparation, response and recovery for small businesses in the pet care industry. The book presents information and is not meant to be a source of legal or insurance advice. The author does not take responsibility for any specific result or lack thereof.

Due to the nature of the Internet, URLs which were accurate at the time this book was published may have changed.

News stories related in the book are summarized from actual pet-related crisis stories. The headlines may have been altered to remove location or business information. A list of news sources can be found in the Resources section.

Each registered trademark mentioned in this book belongs to its respective trademark holder. These products are included as suggestions only and their use does not imply a relationship with the companies involved.

Cover photo source: Peter Daems, Wikimedia Commons
Clipart source: Shutterstock

Sonya Wilson
Southpaws Playschool
2235 South Lamar Boulevard
Austin, Texas 78704

ISBN: 978-0-9978269-0-6

For my parents, George and Vivian Wilson, who gave me a love for animals, an entrepreneurial spirit and a tendency to worry.

ACKNOWLEDGMENTS

Thank you to my pet care industry cheerleaders, Susan Briggs and Charlotte Biggs. Your encouragement means so much to me.

Thanks, John Ratliffe (waspish@gmail.com), for the thorough editing job. I appreciate the restraint that you showed and your diplomatic handling of my dislike of the Oxford comma. Thanks to Kim Roche for the most excellent recommendation of John to edit my first (!) book.

The real life stories added so much to the book. Thanks to those that contributed: Laura Teichmann, Charlotte Petrey, Susan Briggs and Tony Clementi.

My beta readers are greatly appreciated: Jamie Bryan, Catherine Clement, Kelly Cullum, Julie Mendelsohn, Sandy Modell and Elaine Walker. They put the spit in the polish.

Thanks, Mom and Dad, for the $5 garage sale Kindle. It helped a lot.

Most thanks of all to my husband, Tim Smith, who took on most of the work at Southpaws Playschool so that I could spend my time researching and writing. The next one won't be so stressful, I promise.

THERE CANNOT BE A CRISIS NEXT WEEK. MY SCHEDULE IS ALREADY FULL. (HENRY A. KISSINGER)

NOTE FROM THE AUTHOR

I have owned a canine day care since 2002, and my business has faced some "hairy situations." Each time, I rationalized my lack of planning and preparation: there was no extra time, it was too expensive, it was too much trouble, our business was too small to need a plan, and on and on. Finally, I realized that I needed a written crisis response plan so that I could run my pet care business at its optimal level. But as I researched emergency planning for my day care, I kept bumping up against two realities that nearly became roadblocks:

- The disaster planning industry is focused on large office-based corporations. That model did not fit my needs.
- Animal emergency plans focus on family preparedness. That's great, but definitely not the scale on which my business works.

There was no way to use a ready-made template and have it work for me. So I started a process of adaptation and modification of my research that would prepare my employees and my business to overcome any crisis that might arise. Big goal, I know. But I also know that doing something that will move me forward is always better than doing nothing, and so I got started on my plan.

Once I realized that the specific book that I needed to help me create a usable crisis response plan didn't exist, I decided I had to write it. I couldn't leave the subject alone until my plan was in a form that could help others just like me: small business owners in the pet care industry who want the best outcomes for their clients and the animals that have been entrusted to them.

I hope that you will use the information I have gathered to put together your own crisis plan.

Sonya Wilson
Austin, Texas
2016

TABLE OF CONTENTS

PART ONE: INTRODUCTION

GETTING STARTED: CRISIS PLANNING

> **A DISASTER IS A SUDDEN UNPLANNED CALAMITOUS EVENT THAT CREATES AN INABILITY FOR AN ORGANIZATION TO PROVIDE CRITICAL BUSINESS FUNCTIONS FOR AN UNDETERMINED PERIOD OF TIME, RESULTING IN GREAT DAMAGE OR LOSS TO THAT ORGANIZATION. (DEBORAH C. MILLER, 2013)**

The goal of *Hairy Situations* is to help each individual small business owner in the pet care industry put plans and emergency procedures in place to protect lives and livelihood. Even if you have a crisis plan in place for your pet care business, I urge you to read and use *Hairy Situations*. You may find information that you didn't know before, and reading through the sections may spark an idea of how to better prepare your business for crisis situations.

This book is written so that you can read it from cover to cover or skim and use the sections that will help you the most. It contains information on crises ranging from technical failures to life-threatening disasters. When possible, I have included real-life examples of how pet care businesses worked through their own crisis situations.

No one wants to have multiple plans to work through when a crisis strikes. I have sorted through risk management, crisis management, disaster preparation and response, business recovery and business continuity texts and kept the best of the best as it pertains to the pet care industry. The plans and responses included in this book are an "all-hazards approach" designed to help you weather any crisis that comes your way.

You may be wondering how in the world one plan will work for anything and everything that could happen. Your business is unique; no one runs their business exactly the way that you do. Likewise, each imagined crisis and your planned response to it will play a part in the development of your detailed crisis plan binder. Your goal is to plan for the absolute worst-case scenario while hoping for the best outcome.

Crisis mode seems to be the new normal in today's news. The world's increasing population means that property damage and loss of life from natural disasters happens on a larger scale and is therefore being reported more frequently now than in previous years. The range of disasters that can affect your small business is daunting; we will discuss many of them within this text. Any crisis has the potential to affect your business' bottom line. If your software is flawed and you can't correctly process payments, you lose money through sales. A larger disaster, especially one that displaces you from your facility, could close your doors permanently.

Wikimedia/FEMA/Liz Roll

If you are not yet convinced that you need to start writing a crisis plan, think about the ways that having a plan will benefit your business:

- Emergency planning will give your clients and employees a sense of loyalty to your business because they will see your commitment to the safety of the animals entrusted to your care.
- As you work through the planning stage, you will uncover inefficiencies in your processes.
- Streamlined processes will reveal new ways to increase revenue.

- A thorough review (and possible revision) of your insurance policies will enhance your ability to recover from a crisis with no financial loss to your business. A well-written crisis plan could save you money on your insurance premiums as well.
- Fostering a culture of crisis prevention with your employees will encourage them to speak up when they see a situation that is potentially unsafe. This could save you from exposure to liability claims.
- Small actions that you take now to mitigate and prevent disasters could save you from huge outlays on maintenance and upkeep of your facility that could become necessary if such upkeep is delayed or ignored.
- The peace of mind that comes with being prepared for any crisis relieves a lot of your stress as a small business owner. That, as the television commercial says, is priceless.
- A business that has planned for all hazards reduces the drain on the limited resources of first responders and makes that business a better community partner. After you have dealt with your own needs during a community-wide crisis, you will be in a position to offer help to others.

> **THE PLANNING PROCESS WILL IMMEDIATELY BENEFIT YOUR BUSINESS—IRRESPECTIVE OF WHETHER YOUR BUSINESS EVER EXPERIENCES A DISASTER. (DONNA R. CHILDS, 2008)**

Your response to a crisis is only as good as your plan, so plan to stay in business!

By the Numbers

The pet industry has weathered the latest economic downturn and is still growing. According to the American Pet Products Association:

- American consumers spent a record $60.58 billion within the pet industry in 2015
- 65 percent of households in the United States (79 million homes) include pets
- 77.8 million dogs and 85.8 million cats live in U.S. households

And according to the latest available IBISWorld Industry Reports (http://www.ibisworld.com), there is a booming U.S. service industry in place to care for these pets:

- 13,556 pet stores
- 18,144 dog walking businesses
- 48,349 veterinary clinics
- 100,522 pet grooming and boarding facilities

Cintas commissioned Harris Interactive in 2013 to complete a survey of workers' perception of workplace preparedness. In an online survey of 2,019 employed adults:

- 51 percent of workers don't know where their company's first aid kit is located
- 43 percent said that their workplace has an emergency response plan in place
- 31 percent believe that their workplace is proactive about emergency preparedness

The Cintas survey was aimed at corporate America to assess the level of crisis planning, preparedness and employee training amongst potential Cintas clients. How would your employees answer the same questions?

Plan—Train—Practice

Writing a business crisis plan can be compared to buying an insurance policy. Most small business owners have insurance policies that they never use to rebuild their businesses. Yet they still buy those policies because they know that bad things can happen and that they may need to utilize those policies someday in the future.

As a pet care business owner, you have little extra time and few resources to put into creating a crisis plan. Getting started is the hardest part of the project. The second most challenging part of the project is keeping the plan up to date. The files that I have included in the Appendix are meant to help you get started by providing the framework for your plan.

Utilize the assets that you have at hand to complete and implement your plan: delegate appropriate sections of the plan to employees, which will encourage them to take an interest in the planning process.

Once you have evaluated your risks and put your basic plan together, *stop.* Before you put the finishing touches on your disaster binder, it will be extremely helpful to have someone review your plan. None of us can be completely objective when reviewing our own work. Have a colleague who is familiar with the way that your business works look over the rough version and make suggestions, then incorporate any changes into the final version of your plan.

All of your employees should be involved in crisis management planning for your business. Inclusion is integral to making the plan a part of your daily routine. There is no substitute for knowledgeable, dedicated employees, and training becomes much less of a chore if the people that work with you are on board with your plans.

Crisis preparation and response training should be a continual process. Assign someone who has been trained in your facility's crisis management plan to take all new employees through the same steps. Additional training should be provided to each employee who will be expected to take on specialized roles in an emergency.

Hairy Situations

All employees should be familiar with:

- Location of the facility disaster kit and the function of each item in the kit
- Location of fire extinguishers and how to operate them
- Which area of the building will be used for shelter-in-place and how to secure the area for that purpose
- The primary exit for your building and what to do if it's blocked for any reason
- Their roles and responsibilities within the scope of the crisis plan
- What will be expected of them in case of evacuation or shelter-in-place
- The employee contact tree
- Items in the facility emergency pet first aid kit and how to use them
- Emergency policies and procedures (included in your business' crisis plan)
- How to handle animals in stressful emergency situations

Additional options for training:

- At-home disaster planning and preparation
- First aid and CPR
- Emergency pet first aid
- How to turn off building utilities
- The use of your building's alarm system
- How to maintain smoke detectors, carbon monoxide detectors and other safety equipment

Cross-train employees to fill absent or incapacitated workers' roles in a crisis. Since disasters don't follow a timeline, employee cross-training should be done across shifts and across supervisory lines. If someone happens to leave the company abruptly, reassignments are then possible with little or no disruption.

> **THE KEY TO THE SUCCESS OF ANY PLAN IS TRAINING AND TESTING. (ASIS INTERNATIONAL, 2003)**

It does no good to do all of this planning and training and leave it at that. You must practice your emergency action plan—either through tabletop exercises during an all-hands meeting, or, better yet, with real drills in which you and your employees perform the actions that you would take in a crisis situation.

Keep employees prepared with continued training and practice sessions. After each drill, gather everyone together to review what worked and what didn't. Make a sincere effort to correct what didn't work; otherwise, your plan will be become ineffective over time.

CanStockPhoto

PART TWO: LOSS PREVENTION

ASSESS THE THREAT

The events below are frightening just in listed form. Your pet care business could be permanently closed if any of them were to occur. These are just some of the many threats that can affect your business or your community; there are many more. The mistake that most business owners make is to (1) become overwhelmed by the possibilities and never get started on a plan, or (2) become obsessed and spend endless hours working through detailed responses to each of the many causes of business crises.

Animal escape
Animal injury
Arson
Asbestos
Bomb blast
Bomb threat
Brownout
Burst pipe
Cut cable
Chemical spill
CO poisoning
Communications failure
Condensation
Coolant leak
Computer virus
Construction delay
Corrupted data
Cybersecurity breach
Dam failure
Dirty bomb
Dust storm
Earthquake
Economic collapse
Electrical short
Epidemic
Evacuation
Explosion
Faulty sprinkler
Financial difficulty
Fire
Flood
Fraud
Frozen pipes
Hacker
Hailstorm
Hazardous materials
Heatwave
Human error
Hurricane
HVAC failure
Infected data
Infrastructure failure
Insect infestation
Landlord conflict
Landslide
Lightning
Litigation
Loss of key employee
Loss of reputation
Lost data
Mold/mildew
Mudslide
Natural gas leak
Network failure
Nuclear emergency
Oil spill
Personal injury
Pet food recall
Plane crash
Power outage
Power surge
Propane tank explosion
Raw sewage
Relocation
Riot
Road closure
Rodent infestation
Roof cave-in
Sabotage
Sick building
Sinkhole
Smoke damage
Snow storm
Terrorism
Theft/Burglary
Thunderstorm
Toilet overflow
Tornado
Too-rapid growth
Trademark conflict
Train derailment
Transformer fire
Tsunami
Vandalism
Vehicle crash
Volcano
Wildfire
Windstorm
Winter storm
Workplace violence

"Well he certainly does a very thorough risk analysis."

CartoonStock/Shaun McCallig

> You may face a higher risk of man-made disaster if your facility or community is located near a major highway, dam, railroad tracks, a nuclear facility, water treatment plant or chemical-based industry. If you are unsure which risks are the most likely in your area, consult these sources:
>
> Local Office of Emergency Management (OEM)
>
> Local Chamber of Commerce
>
> Insurance Institute for Business and Home Safety (http://www.disastersafety.org)

Think in terms of preparing for various company or community-wide problems, but concentrate on evaluating the risk and probability of damage to your own business. Of course, 100 percent accuracy in predicting which crisis will affect your business is impossible. Some crises, such as power outages, may happen on a regular basis in your area. Other disasters, like a tsunami in Kansas, are quite unlikely. You have the power to protect your bottom line by planning and preparing for the disasters that are the most likely to affect the way you do business.

If your business model wouldn't survive a specific risk, then include that risk in your general contingency plan and spend your time and energy preparing for disasters that your business can survive.

RISK MANAGEMENT

> **AFTER ESTABLISHING THE PROBABILITY OF NEGATIVE EVENTS, YOU WILL NEED TO RATE THEIR POTENTIAL IMPACT AND THEN CREATE APPROPRIATE COUNTERMEASURES. (MICHAEL SEESE, 2010)**

You've identified the most likely crises that could affect your ability to do business, so you've completed the risk assessment stage of your plan. Now you're ready to move on to the risk management phase of preparing your business to survive and thrive. There are four options in risk management:

Prevention: This is my personal favorite of all of the options. Your goal is to keep a specific crisis from happening. An analogy for prevention is replacing a manhole cover to prevent someone from falling into the manhole. Of course, not all crises can be prevented (or even predicted, in some cases), so that's where the other risk management options come into play.

Mitigation: Crises that cannot be prevented can often be mitigated to reduce damage to life and property. Many disaster management planners use prevention and mitigation interchangeably, but these are two separate sections of the risk reduction plan. Mitigation is putting a mattress at the bottom of the manhole to lessen the damage if a person takes a fall.

Transference: Another party assumes the risk for the person's safety. Insurance is the most common form of risk transference. You can insure the manhole cover, or insure the mattress, or buy insurance that would cover any liability. You should insure any item that you cannot afford to lose or replace.

Acceptance: As it turns out, what you thought was a person is actually a cardboard cutout, so let the cutout fall down the manhole. Acceptance is the method of risk management chosen when an item or loss is easily replaceable or of a value that is lower than the cost of insuring it.

Hopefully, your pet care business will never experience a serious facility disaster. Prevention may be the only risk management option that you will ever use. A thorough, continuous prevention program is critical to your business, however, because it involves activities that eliminate the possibility of a disaster. Consider making crisis prevention part of your employees' job descriptions, and be sure to reward outstanding achievement in this area during performance reviews.

PHYSICAL READINESS

Although prevention and mitigation are two separate options in risk management, both are integral to the physical readiness of your business to withstand a crisis. If you have physically prepared your business through prevention and mitigation and have proper insurance in place, you can remain calm during an emergency and focus on what is most important: the humans and animals in your business.

Prevention and mitigation will go farthest if you start with your facility. Whether or not you own your own building, there are actions that you'll want to take that will lead to a safer environment. Start with a detailed look at the structural integrity of the building. Hire a professional building inspector if you don't have experience in this field. Different buildings have different features, but this list should get you thinking about the items that you want the inspector to report on:

- The building's construction type and general condition
- Whether the roof is strong enough to withstand high winds or a heavy snow load
- The presence or absence of hurricane strapping

- Adequacy of insulation in the walls and ceiling
- Evidence of hazardous materials such as asbestos
- Condition of gas mains or propane lines running to the building
- Condition of electrical wiring and whether capacity is sufficient to handle everyday demand
- Potential plumbing issues
- Condition of septic tank
- Heating and air conditioning systems
- Sprinkler system
- Weather assessment of windows and doors
- Site drainage
- Recent building codes that require building improvements
- Other issues that come to the inspector's attention

If you share a building with other businesses, the inspector should report on the condition of the entire building to the extent possible. The condition and maintenance of your neighbors' systems has the potential to directly affect your business and you may need to take mitigating action.

When you get the inspector's report, go over it carefully. Every building inspection report has a list of recommended repairs and improvements. In addition to correcting the structural items that the inspector has flagged, implement non-structural hazard mitigation actions:

Administrative actions:

- Require the use of safety equipment when using power tools
- Prohibit smoking on your property

Physical tasks:

- Add security lighting to the building's outside areas
- Install clearly marked exit signs per your city's building code
- Add a monitored alarm system that includes motion detectors
- Unblock and make all exits accessible
- Install security cameras
- Install smoke detectors and carbon monoxide detectors in appropriate locations
- Consider adding a sprinkler system
- Add transparent film to the inside of windows and glass doors to prevent glass from shattering
- Add an emergency shut-off valve to your propane tank
- Upgrade all surge protectors to UL (Underwriters Laboratories) certified units
- Replace ungrounded plugs with three-prong plugs and outlets (Outlets should be GFCI [ground-fault circuit interrupter] if installed near wet areas)
- Ensure that no more than one appliance is plugged into any extension cord
- Inspect electrical appliances for frayed wires
- Avoid overloading outlets
- Add safety latches to cabinet doors
- Eliminate clutter both inside and outside of the building
- Clear brush and other landscape debris from around the building
- Use hook-and-loop fasteners to keep computers and other equipment secure

- Raise computers, electronic equipment and inventory so that nothing that is sensitive to water damage is at floor level
- Clear spaces around water heaters and furnaces of combustible materials
- Add automatic shut-off valves to your water heater and washing machine
- Add hair traps to your bathing sinks; empty the traps on a regular schedule
- Trim tree limbs away from overhead power lines
- Secure heavy objects (such as bookcases and shelving) to walls
- Install secondary gates or fencing to prevent escape
- Install latches that cannot be opened by animals on gates and doors

Long-term maintenance habits:

- Inspect, clean and repair heating and air conditioning equipment annually
- Follow a strict schedule of filter changes
- Maintain fire extinguishers
- Maintain fans and hair dryers on a regular schedule to keep the motors hair-free

Consider adding a generator to your list of mitigation items if your area is prone to frequent power outages. An appropriately sized and installed generator will enable you to do business as usual in the event you lose power. You'll be able to operate lights and computers and run the heating and air conditioning to keep your employees and the animals in your care comfortable. If your business is in a flood zone, or has a history of being flooded, you will want to have a water pump on hand as well as a generator.

The mitigation and prevention list is extensive. Depending on your situation, you may have more or fewer actionable items. The things that you can complete immediately for little or no cost should be first on your list. Complete the other items on your list as you can. Obviously, the cost of any item should not exceed your potential loss; otherwise, you'll probably decide to accept the risk.

Regular inspections and maintenance of your premises and equipment will lead to a safer environment for the people and animals that enter your building. In the long term, you'll prolong the life of your facility, lower your operation costs and save on your utility bills. It's a win-win situation!

FISCAL READINESS

You can be physically ready for a disaster and have enough insurance to cover every dime of your loss and still lose all that you have worked so hard to build if you run up against delays in claim payment or reconstruction. Fiscal readiness is important to the well-being of your business. Here are some mitigation tactics that you might use:

- Do what you can to build a financial cushion of three to six months' operating expenses. That seems like a lot of money to have "just for emergencies," but it may take that long or even longer to work through a settlement with your insurance company and get customers returning to do business with you. In the meantime, you'll need to use this savings as cash flow.
- Build good credit. If you apply for a low-interest loan after a disaster, your business credit history will be reviewed. If you have set up your business as a sole proprietorship, your personal credit will also be scrutinized.
- Access your free credit reports on a regular basis to be sure that the information is correct.
- Secure optional lines of credit that can be activated if necessary after an adverse event.
- Obtain higher limits on your business credit cards and keep your balances low to preserve spending flexibility.

- Establish a relationship with a bank that will ensure access to capital in the event of an emergency. A good relationship with your mortgage holder may keep you from losing your business: mortgage payments don't stop just because your income stops.

Be sure that your business interruption insurance will reimburse you for payroll policies that you've put in place in case of disaster, such as overtime pay during disaster recovery or continued paychecks in spite of business closure. Few people can afford to lose a paycheck; payroll continuity is important to your employees. Even if your business is not open and has no income, employees have financial obligations to meet and may have disaster-related problems at home.

Small pet care businesses are turning to crowdfunding sites more and more often to raise money for various causes. Crowdfunding is not a substitute for fiscal readiness, but if you have built a large following of loyal customers, then this last-resort idea may be your best chance at recovery in a crisis. Recent examples in the news include the following:

- A dog day care, training and grooming business had been open for sixteen months when it was given just ninety days to vacate the premises so that the building could be torn down. With their original startup debt still being serviced, the owners turned to their clients to help fund the surprise relocation.
- In just thirty minutes, floodwaters completely destroyed and permanently closed a veterinary clinic. Funding was requested to help four employees with bills during their search for new employment.
- A pet store appealed to its customer base to help it stay in business after access to its parking lot had been limited by road construction for more than a year and the store had reached the point of being unable to stock enough inventory to maintain revenue.

BACKUP

Developing technology has allowed increasing numbers of businesses to become almost paperless. Storing documents in "the cloud" is an economical way to control and disseminate data. Data loss, however, is still one of the most common (and costly) crises that small businesses face, mostly due either to a complete lack of backup or to failure of backed-up data.

"He's a whizz at data retrieval."

CartoonStock/Royston-Robertson

As a pet care business owner, you may not take the need for data backup seriously. After all, you can reconstruct customer information, right? But you are required by law to safeguard income tax records and payroll and employee information, and there are serious consequences for not having them on file. You must carefully consider the backup of paper copies of documents as well as documents that are kept on your hard drive.

The best solution for paper documents is to make sure that you have both paper copies and digital copies. Scan documents into files on your hard drive and then print several copies of the scanned documents. Your business disaster binders will have copies of most of your critical business documents. A list of those documents is included in Part Seven.

Don't stop with making copies of your paper documents. According to Quorum.net, the four most common reasons for data loss are (in order of frequency):

- Hardware failure
- Human error
- Software failure
- Natural disasters

Data backup requires some thought on your part:

- Should you perform daily backups?
- Can you back up your data weekly and suffer only a minimum amount of loss if you have to revert to the last backup?
- Will you use an Internet cloud site for data storage?
- Will a portable hard drive, flash drives or CDs suffice to back up your data?
- Does the software program that you use to manage your client and other business data automatically back up? On what schedule?

With more and more business information being carried on laptops, tablets and smartphones, the risk of lost data is higher than ever before. The failure or loss of one of these devices can cause productivity problems for your business. Information that you have stored on portable devices could be unrecoverable if it's not backed up.

Even if you decide to store most of your data online, it's a good idea to get into the habit of regularly downloading information from all of your devices onto alternate media (such as a portable hard drive, CDs or a flash drive) and storing the backup with your offsite disaster binder. This will mitigate the potential for loss, because even online storage is vulnerable to human error.

Untested backup data is the same thing as un-backed-up data. Every version of backup data must be tested before there's a need to rely on it. If you cannot recover your data from your backup media, then you must rely on hard drive recovery efforts, which can cost thousands of dollars—with no guarantee of complete success.

Nolo.com (www.nolo.com) recommends the following document retention periods:

Business income tax returns and supporting documents: Keep the final copy of each year's tax return permanently. Supporting documentation should be kept for seven years.

Employment tax records: Keep a minimum of four years.

Business asset records: Keep records until you have disposed of the asset and the depreciation period is over.

Business ledgers and other key documents: Keep permanently.

Human resources files: Files relating to current employees should be kept for seven years after the employee leaves the company. Records of applicants that were not hired should be kept for at least three years.

Canceled checks: Keep for seven years.

Bank account and credit card statements: Keep for seven years.

DOCUMENTATION

> IF YOU ARE DILIGENT IN YOUR DOCUMENTATION, YOU WILL SMOOTH YOUR PATH TOWARD RECOVERY AND A TIMELY RESUMPTION OF NORMAL OPERATIONS. (BECKY CROW, 2014)

Part of the process of constructing a crisis disaster plan is to streamline your processes and remove clutter, both figuratively and physically. Physical clutter must be removed from your premises for safety reasons and so that you receive all the money you are due if you have to make an insurance claim. Physical clutter makes it harder, if not impossible, for an insurance adjuster to get an accurate list of "fixtures, furniture and fittings." The adjuster will have to guess at the value of the mess that he sees in front of him after a claim has been filed. The adjuster will probably guess low, which is not in the best interest of the business owner.

Once your whole team has worked together to make sure that your business is no longer weighed down with unnecessary items, assign a documentation team. The documentation team's responsibility will be to go from room to room and take high quality pictures of each room and the items in it. As the team moves through a room, they will also compile a written list of all items. Several pictures apiece should be taken of computers and other high value items, and model numbers and other pertinent information noted. Every area of your business should be included.

When the documentation team has completed a first walk-through, photos and written records should be compared to make sure that everything has been included. Any private work areas, such as your desk, can be itemized and added to the record after the team has finished their work.

Now comes the most difficult part of documentation: you must try to locate receipts for the items listed on your inventory. Scan all of the original receipts that you have and include these files with your inventory record. Going forward, when you add a new asset to your business, you'll take a picture, add the item to your inventory list and scan the receipt. Your documentation team can be tasked with list maintenance, with your oversight.

Add copies of both the written document and CDs with all the pictures from the walk-through to your disaster binders. You'll have one copy in each disaster binder for yourself, one for each of the insurance adjusters that you will potentially work with, and one for a public adjuster (if you decide to hire one). The originals should be kept off-site; bring the list to your business on a regular basis to be updated.

If disaster strikes, take detailed photos as soon as you are able after the immediate threat has passed. These "after" photos, along with your inventory photos and written documentation, will show the adjusters exactly what they need to see. If your pictures are clear and you have insured your assets for replacement value instead of actual cost, there should be few problems in getting your claim paid.

INSURANCE

> **INSURANCE IS THE COST OF RECOVERY FROM A CATASTROPHIC EVENT. (MICHAEL SEESE, 2010)**

How much does it cost per day to run your business? Could your business survive if you were forced to close for a week? A month? Could you cover the expenses of rebuilding? If you couldn't recover without financial help, then you must use the strategy of risk transference and insure what you cannot afford to lose.

A study done by The Hartford and published in *Insurance Journal* ("Property and Liability Claims," Apr. 9, 2015) named the top ten most common business insurance claims. Nothing on the list is small potatoes:

- Burglary and theft
- Internal water damage and frozen pipes
- Wind and hail damage
- Building fire
- Customer slipping and falling
- Customer injury and damages
- Product liability
- Physical damage (not weather-related)

- Reputational harm
- Vehicle accident

Disaster prevention and preparedness is the *least expensive form of insurance.* Getting your business ready to survive catastrophic events will stand you in good stead when you start to discuss insurance options with your agent or broker. You will have reviewed your business thoroughly, evaluated your risks and developed a good idea of what your level of coverage should be. You won't run the risk of under- or over insuring your business, which will save you money and aggravation.

For years, it was possible to purchase "pet business insurance" only through professional associations or a few small insurance companies that had the foresight to take on pet care business owners as clients. Lately, mainstream insurance companies have begun to recognize the financial importance of the pet care industry. As a result, more insurers are offering industry-specific coverage. This is helpful from a pet care business owner's perspective, because more competitors in the insurers' market means that better, less expensive coverage is available.

There are two types of insurance salespeople. Agents are responsible for marketing the products of one company (captive agents) or several companies (independent agents). Brokers work with more than one insurance company, but they represent the best interests of the insurance buyer. Both agents and brokers must be licensed to sell insurance.

When you have purchased a policy, you will receive a copy of the whole policy, along with a summarizing cover letter. Do not rely on the cover letter of your insurance policy to tell you what your coverage entails. You, along with your agent or broker, have the responsibility to make sure that you thoroughly understand what you are purchasing before you sign the document. You will be unpleasantly surprised if you need to file a claim and you have misunderstood your coverage for some reason.

Pet care business insurance "must-haves":

- A general liability policy protects against claims made by third parties for physical injury, personal injury or property damage.

- Commercial property insurance covers damage to buildings and their contents due to a covered cause, such as fire. If you rent your building, the property owner often requires being named as a secondary insured party on this policy. Loss of income and extra expenses may be covered under this policy.
- A business owner's policy combines general liability and commercial property insurance at a reduced package rate.
- Extra coverage can be added to your policy as "endorsements" or "riders," and there may be other policies that your business needs for full protection.

Other types of coverage that you might discuss with your agent:

- Animal bailee coverage provides coverage if an animal should become sick or injured or die while in your care.
- A blanket fidelity bond provides coverage for employee theft of money or property from a client.
- Business interruption insurance covers disaster-related expenses that occur until your business operations are fully recovered. It provides for loss of net profits that would have been earned during the disaster period.
- Business vehicle insurance is not covered by the business owner's policy. Your personal vehicle coverage may be sufficient, or you may want to have a policy that covers all vehicles that you or your employees may operate while conducting business.
- Cybersecurity liability covers loss of income from cybersecurity issues and, in cases of stolen client data, covers credit monitoring or other mitigation services that you may have to purchase.
- Employment practices liability covers claims for sexual harassment, discrimination or other illegal business practices that your employees might bring.
- Extra expense covers the amount that you must spend over regular operating expenses to avoid having to shut down after a

covered event. This might include mitigation expenses to prevent further damage, overtime costs for employees, meals, etc.

- Employee dishonesty coverage deals with employee theft of money or property from your business.
- Flood insurance is often excluded from commercial property policies. You can find out if you are eligible for low-cost flood insurance through the National Flood Insurance Program (NFIP) if you're doing business in a vulnerable area.
- Key man insurance is a life insurance policy written for a person involved in the running of your business whose loss would cause a substantial decline in the company's earnings. This policy is meant to provide funds to find and train a replacement for the key employee and to offset income losses due to decreased sales.
- Leasehold interest covers the remaining portion of your lease if your business property is uninhabitable following a covered event.
- Loss of key coverage covers expenses related to losing a client's keys.
- Mobile pet groomer's coverage is a specialty policy that covers your vehicle, equipment and loss of income after a covered event.
- Personal accident coverage provides financial help if the covered person suffers an accident or accidental death.
- Professional liability insurance covers claims made by third parties brought against you as a pet professional. This policy is meant to cover investigation, legal fees, judgments and settlements, whether or not you're found guilty of the action or negligence cited in the claim.
- Umbrella insurance covers a claim against you that is more than the limit of your liability coverage.
- Utility service interruption coverage will cover business losses if you lose electricity because of damage to an electrical substation during a covered event.

- Workers' compensation and disability benefits insurance pays for employees' illness or injuries that occur on the job. It may also help pay for a portion of the affected employee's lost wages. This coverage is mandatory in most states in different forms.

If you need to file a claim, report the loss to your insurance company as soon as possible. Document all damage thoroughly, using video and photo evidence as well as a written account. Keep close tabs on all expenses related to a covered loss event, and train your employees to do the same.

> INSURANCE DISPUTES ARE NOT UNCOMMON FOLLOWING DISASTERS. INSURANCE COMPANIES RELY ON SMALL BUSINESS' RELUCTANCE TO SPEND TIME AND MONEY ON LITIGATION. PROPERLY DOCUMENT THE REPLACEMENT VALUE OF YOUR PROPERTY (AND MAKE SURE THAT YOUR POLICY COVERS YOU THIS WAY) TO AVOID CONFLICT. (DONNA R. CHILDS, 2008)

Review your insurance policies on an annual basis to be sure that they have kept up with the growth and development of your business. Perform the same due diligence with your home insurance policies. Your needs will change over time, and your insurance policies should reflect those changes.

You Can Insure That!

Your insurance agent can write a policy to cover almost any contingency, but you have to make your needs known. If you would like to provide care packages for your employees' families, make wage advances or charge a special rate for the pets that you board during a crisis, let your agent know.

PART THREE:
A LOOK AT REAL LIFE

CRISIS SCENARIOS

If you have been working through the book so far, you have made mighty strides in prevention and mitigation of crises. In this section, we will examine emergencies that you might encounter as a pet care business owner and how these emergencies might be mitigated or prevented. I have used actual news headlines (with identifying information removed) and summarized the responses that the owners of pet care businesses made when their business was confronted with a crisis. Some colleagues have generously chosen to share their disaster stories.

There is no standard threat hierarchy across emergency management: textbooks and response groups don't agree on whether there should be three or four levels, or even how each should be defined. Every crisis, no matter how small it starts, has the potential to close the doors of a small business; therefore, we will study a number of crises that could affect your company or your community, regardless of severity.

COMPANY-FOCUSED CRISES

> EVERYDAY DISASTERS CAN HAVE SERIOUS CONSEQUENCES. (DONNA R. CHILDS, 2008)

The most common crises that affect business activities are localized to a single business. Data loss, broken pipes, power surges and computer crashes are some of the most common events that a business will encounter. Don't discount these and spend less time preparing for them just because they may cause less damage.

Loss of Key Employee

The yearly turnover rate for employees of pet care businesses has been quoted by some sources to be as high as 200 percent. Articles about how to keep employees with you for the long term are published on a regular basis in pet industry trade magazines. Conversely, owners of pet care businesses, probably due to high levels of job satisfaction, are in the profession for the long term: many of you have owned your businesses for ten or more years, and it is not rare to meet people who have owned their businesses for more than thirty years.

REAL LIFE STORY

The pet care industry overall has high job satisfaction rates, but there is also a high rate of burnout due to compassion fatigue. Since we deal with living creatures, it can be hard to distance ourselves emotionally from the animals that we work with.

The pet care industry lost one of the "good guys" on September 28, 2014. Sophia Yin, DVM, focused on teaching pet care providers how to work with animals in a more thoughtful way. Although in many ways Dr. Yin was on top of the world, she suffered from depression and compassion fatigue. Her distress became overwhelming, and she ended her own life.

Dr. Yin put plans in place that allowed her publishing company, CattleDog Press, to survive her passing. Fortunately for all of us, we will be able to continue to learn from Dr. Yin for a long time to come.

Owners are key employees, as are general managers, and company officers. Employees are considered key employees when their departure from the business would disrupt or discontinue business activities. Sometimes what defines a key employee is not a title, but knowledge of the business and how it runs. There are several reasons that key employees might leave the business:

- Resignation or termination of employment
- Personal or family crisis
- Disability due to illness or injury
- Military service
- Death

What would happen to your business if for some reason you could no longer run it? Is there someone that has been trained to take over for you? Are your processes written? What would happen to your business if your most knowledgeable employee suddenly had to leave your employment? In a small business, these are important questions.

> THROUGHOUT YOUR CAREER, THE POSSIBILITY OF SUFFERING A LONG-TERM DISABILITY IS SEVERAL TIMES GREATER THAN THE POSSIBILITY OF DEATH. (DISABILITY INFORMATION RESOURCE CENTER)

Mitigation and Prevention for Loss of Key Person

- Have a contingency plan in place
- Pet sitters, dog trainers and other sole entrepreneurs should be sure to keep excellent records, including their schedule, available in case of emergency
- Draft letters to clients, suppliers and staff that can be used if a tragedy occurs; add these letters to your contingency plan
- Write down your policies and procedures
- Consider purchasing a key man insurance policy
- Purchase a short-term and/or long-term disability policy
- Structure your company so that your business is not forced to close if you die or are disabled; sole proprietorships dissolve when the owners die
- Delegate critical business functions
- Write a will that includes your business and its assets
- Know the law as it relates to employees' long-term leave (Family Medical Leave Act and Uniformed Services Employment and Reemployment Rights Act)

- Develop an extended leave policy
- Cross-train employees so that someone can take over quickly if a key person leaves the company.

HEADLINE

Shock Resignation of Pet Business CEO

Shares in an Australian vet clinic network plummeted after the Chief Executive Officer abruptly resigned. The company mitigated damages by announcing a successor immediately, stressing the replacement's experience and position with the company. The company also announced a rise in profits over the previous year.

Employee Error

THERE IS NO BETTER TEST FOR A PERSON'S CHARACTER THAN HIS OR HER BEHAVIOR WHEN SOMETHING HAS BEEN DONE WRONG. (JUDITH C. HOFFMAN, 2011)

Human error is the single largest cause of workplace emergencies and can result from:

- Poor training
- Poor maintenance
- Carelessness
- Misconduct
- Substance abuse
- Fatigue

Mitigation and Prevention for Employee Error

- Continually hire new employees and keep the best of the best
- Screen potential employees carefully prior to hiring (references check, background check, drug screening)
- Have written work processes available for review
- Put a formal training program in place; have new employees shadow more experienced workers
- Retrain workers if necessary to avoid needless mistakes
- Keep employees mentally present by restricting headphone and cellphone use
- Use positive reinforcement to keep employees motivated to do their best work

HEADLINES

Kennel Give Dogs to Wrong Owners

Two black labs were switched and released to the wrong owners. Neither family knew that they had the wrong dog until the kennel contacted them almost two weeks later. The kennel refunded the boarding fees.

Dog Mauled, Killed by Two Lab-Pit Bull Mix Dogs

A kennel employee mistakenly put a boarding dog into an area where two foster dogs were already present. The two foster dogs attacked and killed the smaller dog. The owner of the kennel put processes in place to make sure there was no repeat of the event.

Financial Difficulty

How do you know it's time to close your business?

- The business is two years old and has not made a profit
- The business was profitable in the past, but has not turned a profit in two consecutive years
- Your health is being negatively affected by constant stress
- Personal relationships have been sacrificed for the sake of the business
- You have lost your passion for what you do

If you still love going to work every day, no matter how hard the struggle, you would benefit from hiring a business consultant who specializes in the pet care industry. The consultant will help you examine your business objectively. You can then make informed decisions about the sustainability of your business and whether it is time for you to move on to other ventures.

Most people who start pet care businesses are pet people, not business people. Marketing, advertising and profit/loss statements are words from a foreign language. It is extremely difficult to make a pet care business work financially while spending ten to twelve hours a day actually working in the business.

You can do everything right, and still run into financial difficulty. Although the pet care industry is growing at a steady rate, small businesses are more vulnerable and have fewer resources than large corporations when a crisis hits and money becomes tight.

Mitigation and Prevention for Financial Difficulty

- Pay down debt before considering opening a pet care business
- Write a solid business plan

- Hire professionals (certified public accountant, payroll administrator) to handle the financial portion of your business
- Take extended learning courses through community college or the Small Business Administration to learn "the language of money"
- Save a financial cushion of three to six months' of operating expenses
- Keep a handle on payroll expenses (percentages should range from about 10 percent of gross revenue for strictly retail to 20-25 percent or more for businesses that are service-oriented)
- Avoid taking on more debt than you can handle
- Be diligent in paying taxes on time
- Insure your business assets properly

HEADLINES

Pet Store Closed Over Tax Questions

The Indiana Department of Revenue closed a local pet store for owing almost $80,000 in back sales taxes. The owner of the business blamed the bad economy.

Family-Owned Pet Store in Tax Crisis Relies on Esprit of Local Economy

A pet store fell behind in paying state income taxes due to a road construction project that slowed down business. When threatened with closure, the owner posted a plea for help on Facebook. Customers bought enough merchandise to pay the taxes that were owed. Finances continued to be a problem until the store closed two years later.

Theft and Fraud

> SMALL BUSINESSES WERE VICTIMIZED IN THE GREATEST PERCENTAGE OF CASES REPORTED TO US, AND THEY SUFFERED DISPROPORTIONATELY LARGE LOSSES DUE TO FRAUD. (ASSOCIATION OF CERTIFIED FRAUD EXAMINERS, 2014)

Theft is costly and often hard to detect. Customer theft is responsible for a large part of retail loss. It is hard to stop a person who is determined to steal from you, but good customer service and well-trained, watchful employees can stop casual thieves just by making them aware they are being watched.

Keep Clients' Credit Card Information Safe

The Payment Card Industry Data Security Standard (PCI DSS) requires that all companies that process, store or transfer client data adhere to a set of security standards designed to keep client information from being obtained and used fraudulently.

Some guidelines that can help you keep information safe:

- Buy and use only validated payment software on your POS equipment or website
- Do not store any sensitive cardholder data on computer files or on paper
- Use a firewall on all of your business computers
- Make sure that your wireless router is password protected and uses encryption
- Use strong passwords
- Teach your employees about security and protecting cardholder data

(Source: the PCI Security Standards Council)

Start your facility security measures by keeping your business clean and clutter-free. A messy, disorganized store gives the impression of carelessness, and may lead a thief to decide that your business is an easy target.

Theft by employees is doubly hard to deal with; you need to be able to trust your employees and employees need to feel that they have your confidence. The best hiring practices and background checks may not be able to completely protect the store from dishonest employees. Regardless of the atmosphere that you try to promote, some employees may exploit weaknesses in your policies and security practices. Factors that contribute to employee theft include:

- Financial—overwhelming bills, gambling debt, addiction
- Perceived mistreatment by management or owner
- Rationalization—they tell themselves they're just borrowing the money and will repay it
- Greed

Mitigation and Prevention for Theft and Fraud

- Greet customers as they enter the business
- Keep the cash register locked when not in use
- Keep animals in view at all times
- Train employees to deal with the various scenarios they may face:
    - Customer shoplifting
    - Theft by other employees
    - Robbery or burglary
- Install security cameras
- Lower displays and shelving to five feet to increase visibility throughout your store
- Make store security a high priority (back doors are locked, deposits made promptly, someone always in the front of the store)

- Leave lights on in your facility after hours, especially if windows face the street
- Provide an area for employees to secure personal belongings
- Train employees on how to recognize fraudulent tactics
- Implement a policy on employee dishonesty that each new hire must read and sign
- Perform mandatory background and reference checks for potential new hires
- Track transactions by employee; patterns become apparent
- Be physically present in your business

HEADLINES

Doggy Day Care Bilked in Scam

A scammer contacted the manager of a dog day care and claimed to be a representative of the energy company. The manager was told that the business' utilities would be disconnected unless $769 was put onto a prepaid debit card and the information was relayed back to the caller within thirty minutes. The manager panicked and did as the caller instructed. The police reported that this is a scam commonly committed against small business owners.

Police Nab Suspect for Pet Store Robbery

The owner of a pet store was held at gunpoint while the robber emptied the cash register. Surveillance photos of the man were published on social media, online and on television; citizen tips led to the man's arrest. The man was caught on camera robbing a pizza restaurant and a hospital cafeteria the same day.

Workplace Violence

UNDER THE OCCUPATIONAL SAFETY AND HEALTH ACT, EMPLOYERS HAVE A DUTY TO FURNISH A SAFE AND HEALTHFUL WORKING ENVIRONMENT FOR THEIR EMPLOYEES. (KENNETH N. MYERS, 2006)

Workplace violence is not just the act or threat of physical violence. Harassment, intimidation or other threatening behavior that occurs at a place of employment is also considered workplace violence. It ranges from verbal abuse to homicide. Workplace violence can involve management, employees, clients or even outside parties. According to OSHA (Occupational Safety and Health Administration), homicide is the leading killer of women in the workplace.

Mitigation and Prevention for Workplace Violence

- Write a zero tolerance harassment and violence policy
- Dismiss employees who violate your written policy
- Install security cameras
- Install low illumination lighting on the exterior of your building to make it safer for employees to walk to their cars at night
- Perform background checks, reference checks and drug screening for potential new employees
- Establish work schedules that will encourage cohesive teams
- Reward effective teamwork
- Provide employees with training in situational awareness and self-protection
- Write protocols for building security and personal safety
- Train supervisors in how to defuse stressful and potentially violent situations

- Pay attention to the quality of relationships among staff members
- Model acceptance of individual differences
- Open lines of communication among owner, management and staff
- Establish code words to indicate that a customer or other party may become violent

HEADLINES

Pet Store, Former Manager Sued for Sexual Harassment, Wrongful Termination

A woman sued a pet store and a former manager of the store in federal court, claiming that she was sexually harassed and inappropriately touched. She also claimed that she was threatened with bodily harm and shortened work hours if she reported the abuse. The manager pleaded guilty to misdemeanor assault charges. The woman was terminated by the pet store for extended absences from work. The suit alleged the pet store was responsible for fostering a hostile work environment.

Police: Man Attacked Pet Shop Owner in Grooming Dispute

A man brought his dog into a grooming shop and requested that the dog be shaved everywhere except its ears. When the groomer brought the dog's matted ears to the man's attention and said they would have to be shaved for the health of the dog, the man got angry and hit the groomer and one of her employees in the face. The man was arrested for the assault.

Animal Escape or Loss

One of the greatest fears that most of us as pet care business owners have is that an animal will escape or be lost while under our supervision. Our clients believe that they are leaving their pets in capable hands and that the animals will be kept safe while they travel. However, even though we are paid professionals and should be using extra care, sometimes an animal gets loose. A desperate, quick thinking animal will exploit any opportunity for escape.

Mitigation and Prevention for Animal Escape

- Post prominent signs on gates and doors that must remain closed
- Have at least two gates or doors between an animal and the outside world
- Train employees in proper gate management
- Make use of an airlock at entrances to slow clients and enhance awareness
- Ask clients directly whether an animal is prone to escape; make employees aware of "escape artists"
- Use strategies to minimize anxiety in your facility
- Require that dogs keep collars and tags on while in group play; if that is not possible for safety reasons, make sure that play collars with your business' contact information are worn
- Keep fences and gates in good repair
- Add tops to outdoor kennel spaces so that escape artists can be boarded safely
- Ensure that all latches are escape proof (dogs as well as other animals have been known to open latches)
- Reptile terrariums, herpetariums and small mammal habitats should be securely lidded
- Separate bird cages from loose dogs and cats in the home; make sure the cage is secured with a bird-proof latch
- In-home caregivers should enter client's homes carefully to prevent door dashes
- Use non-slip collars (martingales), slip leads or properly fitting harnesses when walking dogs

- Supervise animals closely while they are in a group setting (dog play yards, catteries)
- Count animals frequently throughout the day or at each visit to make sure that all are present

HEADLINES

Kennel Loses Woman's Beloved Cat

A woman took her cat to be boarded for two days. The first morning that the cat was in the kennel, an employee propped open the door to the building. When the staff member opened the cat's cage to clean the litter box, the cat jumped out of the cage and ran out the front door in seconds.

The staff of the kennel baited a trap in the area in hopes that the cat would be returned to its owner.

Family Searching for Dog Who Escaped From Boarding Kennel

Three dogs went missing from a kennel while their owners were on vacation. Two of the dogs were recovered, but the owners of the third dog believe that she was most likely hit by a car and killed, since she loved to chase cars.

The dogs escaped when one of the dogs opened latches for himself and two others. The kennel owner said that the dog was known to be a latch flipper, but that knowledge was not passed on to the managers at the time the dog was boarded. The dogs got out of the kennels, pushed open the door to the play yard, flipped the latch on the play yard and left the property through a faulty automatic gate.

The kennel's owner placed locks on all of the kennel doors to prevent a repeat of this tragedy.

Fire

Fire ranks among the costliest causes of commercial property damage. Since fires in pet care business facilities almost always result in loss of the lives of the animals that are in the facility, it is especially important that everything possible be done to avoid being susceptible to this devastating risk. Fires in commercial buildings are most often caused by failure of the electrical wiring system. Other risks include:

- Cooling and heating malfunctions
- Smoking
- Natural gas leaks
- Improper storage
- Worn electrical cords
- Overloaded electrical systems
- Appliance or other equipment failure
- Lightning strike
- Arson

Fire Mitigation and Prevention

- Create an emergency evacuation plan
- Hold regular training and drills for employees
- Install a sprinkler system
- Install a remote alarm system
- Install smoke and carbon monoxide detectors
- Install a lightning suppression system
- Keep fire extinguishers fully charged

- Designate your business a non-smoking facility
- Conduct regular building inspections
- Schedule a fire department inspection; follow recommendations
- Do not run portable fans or dryers without supervision
- Add overnight attendants to your work schedule

If the worst happens, and your facility is affected by fire, monitor the health of all animals closely for several days, especially the very old and very young. Amphibians, reptiles and birds are extremely sensitive to smoke. Animals may not display overt symptoms of injury suffered during the fire for several days. Watch for signs of distress brought on by emotional trauma as well.

> Fireproof safes must be rated to UL125 to protect any data storage media. That means that the inside of the safe did not heat higher than 125 degrees Fahrenheit in UL (Underwriters Laboratories) testing.

HEADLINES

Veterinary Clinic Recovering from Deadly Fire

A fire that killed nine dogs in a veterinary clinic was found to be caused by an electrical problem. The owner had performed regular building maintenance. The clinic was closed for five weeks. Complete rebuilding took a year and a half.

The clinic was well-insured. During the closure and rebuilding, employees were kept busy with cleanup, painting and other tasks.

City Considering Code Changes Following Two Devastating Fires at Pet Businesses in Six Months

Lawrence Journal-World/Mike Yoder

After fires at two pet businesses within six months, city commissioners discussed changes to building codes for animal facilities. Fire codes do not currently require special features for businesses that house animals.

Both fires caused significant loss of animal life. Neither business had a fire sprinkler system or a monitored alarm. One fire was caused by a fault in the main breaker panel, the other by a seized motor in a box fan. The fires were called in by bystanders who noticed smoke coming from the businesses.

In September, commissioners agreed to require all animal housing facilities to install smoke and carbon monoxide remote monitoring systems, as well as be equipped with fire extinguishers and provide extinguisher training for staff, plus create emergency plans and drills for staff.

Injuries

> **WHETHER OR NOT YOU OWN THE PROPERTY, YOU ARE RESPONSIBLE FOR THE SAFETY OF YOUR CLIENTS, EMPLOYEES AND ANYONE ELSE WHO MAY BE ON THE PREMISES. (NEIL BAUM AND JOHN W. MCDANIEL, 2009)**

We work with animals every day. We try our best, but accidents will happen. It's the nature of the business that we are in. Animals can be unpredictable. They have sharp teeth and claws. Sometimes pets don't want to do what we want them to: stand still for an examination or a groom or play nicely with each other. Injuries are expensive to your bottom line and to your reputation.

ShutterStock

Injury Mitigation and Prevention

- Use appropriate tools for the job at hand to prevent injury
- Know your profession's best practices guidelines and follow them
- Train staff members in pet emergency first aid and CPR

- Train staff members in animal behavior
- Do not leave animals unsupervised
- Draft waivers and release forms that will hold up if challenged in court
- Set policies that protect the animals in your care
- Do not allow small children into off-leash play areas, and do not allow children to pick up or handle animals
- Carry both general liability and professional liability insurance policies
- Carry workers' compensation and disability insurance
- Assess each animal coming in to your care for illness or pre-existing injuries
- Practice proper restraint and containment protocols at all times
- Keep first aid kits on hand for both pet and human injuries
- Write a policy that addresses under what circumstances your business will pay a veterinary or medical bill
- Be ready to refund money for services rendered if an animal is injured while in your care
- Be honest about the cause of any injury. Document with photos if possible
- Take responsibility for injuries that happen on your premises
- Show empathy for the injured person or pet

HEADLINES

Man Sues Pet Shop after Slipping on Dog Feces

A man slipped on a pile of dog feces and hurt his back. He also struck his head, knocking out four of his false teeth. He sued the business for $1 million. He stated in his lawsuit that the store's employees were negligent in not cleaning the feces from the floor before he stepped in it.

The store maintained that it was not liable for the man's injuries, since it provided supplies for pet owners to clean up after their own animals and trained its employees to be diligent in cleaning the store of pet waste.

Dog, Employees Suffered Injuries at Doggy Day Care Site

A small dog was killed when an employee at a dog day care let large dogs into a pen containing smaller dogs. The kennel owner was accused of trying to cover up the dog's death by saying that the dog died a natural death. Employees allegedly were told to lie about the incident.

Veterinarians at a nearby clinic said that they had to treat several dogs from the day care that suffered bite wounds and severe cuts.

Two former employees of the dog day care filed workers' compensation suits. One employee was bitten on the face and arm and required five stitches. The other employee was bitten on the hand while breaking up a fight and accrued over $30,000 in medical bills.

HVAC Failure

When properly cared for, air conditioning and heating units are wonderful things. It's nice to be able to go to the thermostat on the wall and make the climate change. We cannot forget that commercial HVAC (heating, ventilation and air conditioning) failures are common and that failure usually happens during the time when demand is greatest.

Reasons why HVAC systems fail:

- Accumulation of debris around the unit
- Improper installation
- Lack of maintenance
- Improper size of unit versus demand

HVAC Failure Mitigation and Prevention

- Pet sitters should understand how to operate clients' heating and air conditioning units
- Plan alternative ways to keep animals cool or warm in case of unit failure
- Keep the condenser coil clean
- Keep debris and brush from building up around condenser unit
- Protect condenser unit from exposure to pet urine, chewing and digging
- Secure unit against theft (thieves can strip the unit of valuable copper wiring in minutes)
- Follow a strict filter replacement schedule
- Purchase units with the proper capacity to avoid overwork
- Hire a certified professional to check units at least yearly

HEADLINES

Pet-Store Animals Saved After Condenser Fails During Heat Wave

The rooftop HVAC condenser failed at a pet store. Temperature and humidity began to rise. The pet store used fans to keep animals cool and moved the largest animals to another store. No animals were lost during the episode, although the temperature inside the store reached 97 degrees.

The city, the local utility company and the store owner worked together to get a new unit installed in about thirty six hours. The job was given priority because of the animals' need. A crane was rerouted from another city to install the new condenser unit.

Workers, Animals Evacuated From Pet Store After Gas Leak

St. Louis Post-Dispatch/Robert Cohen

A suspected refrigerant gas leak at a pet store sent seven people to the hospital. A few hours after the air conditioner stopped working, people started complaining of nausea and dizziness. Multiple animals were evacuated, and the store closed until the air conditioning units could be evaluated and repaired. The evacuated animals were housed in a Metro bus until they could be returned to their owners or moved to temporary shelter.

Computer or System Failure

Power surges are the most common danger to electronic equipment. Often lasting only a millisecond, power surges cost the US economy billions of dollars in damage every year. The problem is often internal, as opposed to a problem with the power utility.

Other reasons behind system failure are varied:

- Poor quality or age of computer hardware
- USB or hardware incompatibility
- Upgrades that are incomplete or poorly performed
- User error
- Bugs in newly installed software
- Physical damage to hardware
- Malware, spyware, viruses

A computer failure includes more than just hardware. A server failure at your Internet service provider (ISP) could cause problems, as could newly installed software that is being used by inadequately trained operators.

Although many pet care businesses are dependent on computers for daily activities, most could survive during a relatively short period without a computer. The key is to devise alternative plans to accommodate the most critical activities of your business. These plans will be less efficient, but keeping sales, payroll and other identified transactions going will prevent you from closing your doors when the computer becomes a doorstop.

> **THE DIFFICULT PART IS FOCUSING ON THE RIGHT ISSUE—KEEPING THE BUSINESS RUNNING RATHER THAN KEEPING THE COMPUTER RUNNING. (KENNETH N. MYERS, 2006)**

Mitigation and prevention for computer system failure

- Insure equipment that you cannot afford to lose
- Backup data on a regular basis
- Verify that data backups are usable
- Add surge protectors for sensitive equipment
- Control the temperature where computers and other electronic equipment is used
- Keep pet hair or dander from blocking computer cooling vents
- Store PIN information and credit card numbers under lock and key (or under several layers of security if they're on your computer system)
- Have an alternate strategy for processing sales transactions if your business is without access to the Internet
- Write a policy that addresses Internet usage to minimize the chance of invasion by malware, spyware and viruses
- Have a strict computer hygiene policy—no downloads or programs that are not approved by management
- Install a high-quality computer security program and put appropriate firewalls in place
- Keep software licenses and disks available for reload on short notice
- Utilize email and other Web-based services that are not dependent on a specific computer
- Train computer users on new software
- Incorporate loss of Internet and phones into your crisis plans
- Have an IT professional regularly assess your computers' security weaknesses

Legal Issues

Median Costs of Litigation by Case Type

- Automobile $43,000
- Premises liability $54,000
- Real property $66,000
- Employment $88,000
- Contract $91,000
- Malpractice $122,000

Source: Court Statistics Project, 1/1/2013

Being threatened with a lawsuit is a crisis in itself. As a pet care business owner, litigation can hit you from anywhere: disgruntled clients, fired employees, partners or landlords. The high cost of legal action prevents most threats from coming to fruition; however, the stress can be overwhelming.

Mitigation and prevention for legal issues

- Carry both business liability and professional liability insurance
- Know the best practices for your profession and follow them
- Hire people with a high level of integrity
- Retain an attorney who specializes in small business law to write or review contracts
- Know your state's laws regarding liability, waivers and employee contracts
- Draft customer waivers that cover all contingencies
- Suggest binding arbitration to the other party in a lawsuit if that is a better option for your business

- Consider using a non-solicitation agreement instead of a more restrictive non-compete clause in your employee contracts
- Protect your brand with trademark registration

HEADLINES

A Sick Cat, a Big Bill, and a Lawsuit

A kennel owner took a sick cat to an emergency medical center when it fell ill while being boarded. The cat's owners were upset that the cat was not taken to its own veterinarian, where the bill would have been lower. The cat's owners sued the kennel owner for the emergency veterinary bill, which was $3,861. The judge in the case found that the kennel owner acted reasonably in taking the cat to the emergency veterinarian.

Head of a Dog Boarding Business is Suing Her Ex-Colleague

A dog day care owner accused a former colleague of opening a competing lodging, grooming and training business using the dog day care's client information database. The new business was established within the boundaries of the non-compete agreement that the two parties signed. The lawsuit demanded $50,000 in damages and relocation of the competing facility.

Facility Damage

LOSING YOUR PHYSICAL SPACE CAN BE TERRIBLE AND CAN DESTROY YOUR BUSINESS. CUSTOMERS HAVE BUILT A ROUTINE AROUND COMING TO ONE LOCATION AND THE DISRUPTION IS DIFFICULT. (ETHAN CROWTHER, 2013)

Like a bolt of lightning, property damage can hit a business right out of the blue. Whether damage happens as the result of an accident, a weather event or malicious intent, having a plan in place can help you get back into business quickly.

Mitigation and prevention for facility damage

- Do not return animals to the facility until the damage is repaired and construction cleanup has been completed
- Have infrastructure inspected prior to repairs
- Know what your property insurance excludes

If your business premises has suffered extensive damage, consider whether relocation is a better option than reconstruction: new construction or remodeling often moves more quickly than rebuilding. Identify possible hazards when searching for a new location, e.g., railroad crossings, water treatment plants, nuclear facilities, flood plains. At least one fire hydrant should be within sight of the new location.

HEADLINES

Sewage Backup Damages Dog Training Facility

A sewage backup severely damaged a new service dog training facility. The group moved into its new facility on August 7th and ten days later it was flooded with four inches of sewage. The flooding ruined floors and walls, totaling almost $150,000 in damages.

The sewage problem was the result of a block on the city's main line. The state's insurance reserve fund covered only a basic cleanup and disinfection. The service group's insurance had an exclusion for sewage backups, which organizers were not aware of until the problem occurred.

A service district representative said that the sewage backup into the kennel could have been prevented with a backflow preventer. The kennel is closed until funds can be raised to complete repairs.

Redding Record-Searchlight/ZUMAPRESS.com/Dylan Darling

Car Crashes Into Dog Grooming Shop

An elderly woman accidentally drove her car deep into her dog groomer's glass storefront. The crash caused about thirty thousand dollars' worth of damage. The front counter was pushed more than twenty feet into the building.

A customer and a dog groomer were slightly injured in the crash. The driver of the vehicle was shaken up, but not hurt. None of the dozen dogs in the shop were harmed. Groomers continued to work on completing grooms while cleanup started.

Loss of Reputation

Reputations in the pet industry are built on trust. Clients trust you to properly care for their animals and keep them safe; you are trusted to give the right information or sell safe products. What can you do when that trust is shattered and your reputation has gone with it?

> **IT TAKES TWENTY YEARS TO BUILD A REPUTATION AND FIVE MINUTES TO RUIN IT. IF YOU THINK ABOUT THAT, YOU'LL DO THINGS DIFFERENTLY. (WARREN BUFFETT)**

It's not easy to rebuild a bad reputation. Regaining the public trust takes a lot of time and effort. It has been proven many times that the public can forgive and forget if the business honestly admits that it was in the wrong and takes steps to correct the problem.

Mitigation and Prevention for Loss of Reputation

- Include reputation management in your crisis management plan
- Be aware of what is being said about your business through regular media channels as well as on social media. Google Alerts is a good tool for this task
- A negative review can be a good thing if you respond in the right way; it makes you look human and real
- Keep your perspective. Not everyone is going to love you, no matter how hard you try
- Have all business permits, licenses and certificates of occupancy in place; after any incident the media will search public records to find irregularities in your business practices
- Be contrite, apologize sincerely, take responsibility
- There is no room for defensiveness if your business is in the wrong
- Employees must be on board with your attempts at reputation rebuilding
- Be as open as possible about what you are doing to fix the problem
- Adopt new policies that will prevent a repeat of what caused your negative reputation and do not allow a recurrence
- Emphasize the importance of the health and safety of the animals in your care
- Give honest, solid information that the public can believe

- Do not hide behind "no comment"; otherwise, what your critics say will be perceived as true

Focus on re-establishing yourself in the community. Go back to the basics: ask yourself what it was that made your business' good reputation. Positive actions will go a long way towards forgiveness. A business that was well-run and successful prior to a single negative event has a better chance at recovery than a business that has a poor reputation. In the latter case, it might be better to rebrand your business, relocate or start over with another venture.

REAL LIFE STORY

A Cautionary Tale

Twenty-three dogs died while being boarded at a kennel in June, 2014. Some of the facts of the incident:

- The owners of the kennel went on vacation across country without notifying clients, leaving two young adults in charge of over thirty dogs and five small children
- Twenty-eight dogs were shut in a room that was less than 150 square feet
- An HVAC expert reported that the air conditioner was inadequate for its intended purpose and catastrophically failed due to a dirty air filter
- The dogs died of what was likely hyperthermia and lack of oxygen

At least three Facebook groups and countless media articles address this disaster. The kennel owners steadfastly maintained that the deaths were a horrible accident and that they were innocent of any wrongdoing.

In June, 2016, the kennel owners were offered and accepted a plea deal. Each of them pled guilty to one count of fraud and one count of animal cruelty/neglect. Each will serve a short jail sentence and probation and may not hold any position working with animals.

The takeaway from this story: This was not an accident. Poor planning, lack of training, inadequate staffing and negligence became a tragedy for all concerned.

HEADLINES

Doggy Day Care Halts Use of Muzzles

The owner of a dog day care said muzzles would no longer be used after concerns were raised over how the dogs were treated. The owner released a statement saying that muzzles were only used occasionally; however, a former employee reported to news media that the facility's owner required the use of muzzles to prevent barking; the dogs were muzzled for hours and sometimes overnight. Signs were posted in the facility directing employees to keep dogs muzzled at all times.

Dog Business Involved in Pet's Death Cited by State

The owners of a home boarding facility reported to a dog's owners that their dog had escaped from the facility's yard. The dog's owners spent two months searching for their dog before being told the truth: the dog had been attacked and killed by the owner's dog and the kennel owners had lied about the incident. The business was cited for operating a boarding kennel without a license by the state and closed.

COMMUNITY-WIDE DISASTERS

> WHEN DISASTER STRIKES, YOU MAY BE ON YOUR OWN FOR SEVERAL HOURS, SEVERAL DAYS OR EVEN WEEKS. EMERGENCY SERVICES MAY NOT BE ABLE TO RESPOND RIGHT AWAY. (NEIL BAUM AND JOHN W. MCDANIEL 2009)

Fortunately, disasters that affect an entire community are less common than events that affect just one business. Even so, plans and preparation will save lives and help you get on the fast track to business recovery. Be community-minded; network with your business neighbors to find out whether they have made plans to handle a disaster and encourage them to do so if they haven't yet started.

Push Client Preparedness

Along with getting your business prepared to weather any crisis, encourage your clients to become personally prepared to take care of themselves and their pets in a disaster.

There are many excellent checklists and brochures available, as well as courses that you can suggest:

The Department of Homeland Security (https://www.ready.gov) provides a month by month schedule of readiness activities that you can promote

The American Veterinary Medical Association (www.avma.org) has produced a brochure, *Saving the Whole Family,* that is available for free download or in print for a nominal fee

The Center for Food Security and Public Health at Iowa State University maintains a website and has a booklet available for download to prepare rural communities for all hazards (http://www.prep4agthreats.org/)

The Federal Emergency Management Agency (FEMA) offers a course to educate the public on preparedness issues. The course is titled IS-22 Are You Ready? An In-depth Guide to Citizen Preparedness (http://www.training.fema.gov/)

A good place for you to get started with mitigation and prevention for community-wide emergencies is your city or county office of emergency planning. In some locations, the county emergency services office has been merged with Homeland Security and Emergency Management (HSEM) offices, and some counties have maintained separate office and planning functions. Your county office or regional HSEM has already done a hazard identification and vulnerability analysis for the most likely hazards in your area.

Know whether your community has some sort of "reverse 911" communications plan to allow emergency services to give homes and businesses advance notice of weather, wildfire or other conditions that would require the public to take action. If so, register both your business number and your cell phone number. Encourage all of your staff members and clients to register for this free service as well.

When a regional disaster happens, one of the first things to break down is cell phone communication, since networks will quickly become overwhelmed with calls. It may be easier to make long-distance phone calls than local ones during a disaster. Designate a "relay caller" that is at least one hundred miles from your business' location. This caller can both receive calls and call into the devastated area to make contact with employees and clients until the local network is clear again.

Wildfire

Wildfires are happening more frequently and burning hotter than ever before. As built-up areas encroach on wild areas, more damage is being done to homes and businesses by wildfire. Know the potential for wildfires in your area, stay on top of the news and make preparations to deal with a fire if you are faced with this situation.

Mitigation for Wildfire

- Build or retrofit your facility to withstand both high temperatures and actual fire
- Keep vehicles on the premises with enough capacity to hold all animals in one trip
- Train employees to drive each of the vehicles they may be asked to operate
- Evacuate at the first sign of fire or first warning
- Invest in firefighting equipment if you are in a rural area that is at high risk of wildfire
- Never leave the premises unattended if animals are present

REAL LIFE STORY

The most memorable moments in our lives include the worst of times and the best of times. Either way, they become milestones that will be remembered throughout our lifetime. The tragedy that unfolded on February 27, 2011, was one that Laura Teichmann will never forget. Laura's life-changing experience has given her a chance to help make a difference in how we view evacuation plans and being well prepared. This is Laura's story:

It was a typical Sunday morning, consisting of homemade breakfast and family bonding. As the day proceeded, I remember looking outside and thinking *This kind of wind is unnatural at this time of year* but not much more. As we gathered in the living room later that day, my daughter got an update on Facebook and asked if we knew about the fire. As soon as I heard the word "fire," a mixture of emotions ran through my body. Mostly I was scared.

Our kennel was located in the backyard and I was worried about the fire spreading, so I informed the kennel employees of the situation in case we were forced to evacuate. Fear started spreading through my employees as they gathered the animals in the van. Now I began to imagine the worst possible things that could happen. My family was at home trying to get our animals to the vehicles. While we were loading the animals I quickly came to realize that the van was not big enough to fit all of the animals we had that day.

I tried to get a mile down the road to my mom's house to retrieve our motor home, but was forced to turn back halfway there due to the fire spreading in our neighborhood. In my moment of desperation I tried to fit as many dogs as I could in the van. At this point you may ask why I didn't have more help or why I didn't just leave. Four years later, I still can't fully answer those questions, but I can emphasize the importance of safety.

When a fire burns out of control like it did on that fateful day, first responders block off the area and NO ONE is allowed in. I was so limited as to what I could do at that moment. The majority of my staff was at the evacuation exit site, begging the first responders to go in and help with the animals. With the first responders there, I knew my employees were in good hands. What the first responders did that day was lifesaving.

In times of disaster we sometimes see heroes rise to a call for help. My aunt was blocked from getting to her house to save her animals, and yet in this moment of fear and anguish she stopped to help us load animals into the van. We loaded nearly twenty animals. Once her vehicle was full, she headed out to get them to safety.

I kept going back to get as many animals out as I possibly could, until my husband stopped me and told me the sheriff was forcing us to evacuate. At that moment I knew I could still save more dogs. I turned back around and when I came outside the sheriff was standing there telling me if I didn't leave now, he would be forced to make me leave.

AP Photo/The Amarillo Globe News/Michael Schumacher

The first responders did all they could to try and rescue the remainder of the animals in the kennels. We are forever grateful for all they did, letting the animals loose and hoping that they would reach safety. Animal control also arrived and loaded up a dozen more animals and removed them safely from the fire zone. Owners were desperately stopping some of the trucks in hopes that their beloved family members were safe. Overall, the first responders were able to pull out twenty-four more animals that we were unable to retrieve. We got them to another kennel where we could offer them medical care. Everyone who helped that day was a hero and we are forever grateful.

Wildfires are devastating, especially when they move into an inhabited area. After everything was over, we had lost eighteen pets. Their memorial stands in trees planted around our new business, but the truth is, there isn't a day that goes by that I don't think about those animals. The tragedy that those families had to endure that day was heartbreaking. That was the hardest week of my life. I think of them often.

We were blessed to have above-and-beyond-glorious clients whose non-stop calls of concern and care helped us get through this terrible tragedy. Their faith in me and endless acts of kindness will never be forgotten. They helped us get our lives back by assisting in cleanup, offering prayers, and searching outlying areas looking for the pets that were set free. And the thing that started the healing process was knowing I was needed and that people were asking us when we would reopen again.

As we began the mounting work of figuring out what to do next and trying to reassemble our lives, our clients wanted to help us by bringing back their dogs for grooming and care. So a week later, on Sunday, we started the healing process in a borrowed grooming shop working with the dogs we love. I believe we did twelve dogs that day, but ever since, we have been up and running! My faith saw me through and made me believe that we could do this. The world challenged me that day and God helped me through. The reason I am sharing the events that unfolded February 27, 2011, is because I want to share the knowledge I gained from these circumstances.

I want to stress the importance of having an evacuation plan in place and installing safety measures in your salons. Through life there are ups and downs, and along with those ups and downs come challenges, which sometimes we are not fully prepared for. Even though every precaution is taken and every plan is made, tragedy can strike at the most unlikely of times. Be prepared!

Set standards in your salon and live up to those standards. As a pet care professional, be the best that you can. Establish a caring business that is safe for everyone. Know that you always do your best!

I hope my story has helped to be a stepping stone for what we desperately need in this industry: A working community with values and ethics that help move us forward.

A friend of mine once said, "Know your groomer, and ask questions, and don't let the first question be price." We know the value of safety and it's up to you to decide how much that is worth.

Laura Teichmann, Willow Creek Kennels

Earthquake and Tsunami

> EVEN WITH ALL OUR TECHNOLOGY AND THE INVENTIONS THAT MAKE MODERN LIFE SO MUCH EASIER THAN IT ONCE WAS, IT TAKES JUST ONE BIG NATURAL DISASTER TO WIPE ALL THAT AWAY AND REMIND US THAT, HERE ON EARTH, WE'RE STILL AT THE MERCY OF NATURE. (NEIL DEGRASSE TYSON)

Earthquake is a risk wherever there is a fault line in the earth's crust. A tsunami (wave of sea water) occurs after an earthquake or other abrupt, violent movement of the ocean floor.

In the July 20, 2015, issue of *The New Yorker,* an article called "The Really Big One" discusses the probability of the next very big earthquake. Scientists have predicted that an earthquake will destroy a large portion of the coastal Northwest. The odds of a big earthquake happening in the northwestern United States within the next fifty years has been determined to be one in three.

The area that scientists believe will be affected is home to over seven million people. FEMA estimates that nearly one million buildings in the area will collapse or be compromised in the quake. The earthquake will likely be followed, scientists say, within fifteen to thirty minutes by a tsunami that will vary from twenty to over one hundred feet high.

Mitigation for Earthquake and Tsunami

- Know your risk level
- Locate your business away from high-risk areas
- Train your employees on how to protect themselves during the most likely events
- If you are building a new building, implement earthquake-resistant design

Weather-Related Events

Each year, businesses suffer billions of dollars in damage from weather-related natural disasters: floods, hurricanes and tornadoes. The Center for Research on Epidemiology of Disasters categorizes an event as a natural disaster if it kills ten or more people, displaces more than one hundred people or is categorized by the affected country as a disaster.

In the United States, tornadoes usually occur during March through August. Hurricane season is generally mid-August to October. Weather forecasters use the words "usually" and "generally" because both events can happen any time of the year if conditions are favorable. Weather events can also happen in combination. A thunderstorm can cause such heavy rains that flooding occurs, or a hurricane's storm surge can devastate a community.

Weather Words (Source: NOAA, 2/28/2014)

A watch lets you know that weather conditions are favorable for a hazard to occur. It means "Be on guard!" During a weather watch, gather awareness of the specific threat and prepare for action. Monitor the weather to find out if severe weather conditions have deteriorated and prepare to take shelter.

A warning requires immediate action. This means a weather hazard is imminent: it is either occurring (a tornado has been spotted, for example) or it is about to occur. Find safe shelter immediately.

Mitigation and Prevention for Weather-Related Events

- Register for reverse 911 notification on business and cell phones
- Pay attention to news and weather reports
- Do all that you can to be physically ready well before the event
- Encourage employee and client home preparedness
- Install a lightning suppression system

- Carry property insurance that covers the cost of replacing your business contents
- If you are in a flood-prone area, carry a flood insurance policy; most other policies exclude flood damage
- Purchase a generator that will power your most urgent business functions
- Record pets' microchip numbers to facilitate reuniting animals and their owners
- Require "no-fail" pickup numbers from all of your clients
- Be prepared for loss of communication and utilities (including water) after a disaster
- Keep your vehicle's gas tank at least half full at all times
- If you are forced to evacuate:
    - Do not wade or drive through moving water. One to two feet of water can sweep a car away
    - Watch for downed power lines
    - Check for fire hazards, gas leaks or damaged electrical wiring before returning to the building

HEADLINE

Resilient Breed of Business: Dog Mom's Pet Boarding Reopens After May Tornado

A pet grooming and boarding business that was destroyed by tornado reopened after a six-month rebuilding job. The new building was constructed with concrete and reinforced rebar and included a storm shelter. The original building was leveled, but all of the twenty dogs in the kennel were found and returned to their owners. Most stayed near the kennel, but some were found across the street and others were in a nearby field.

REAL LIFE STORY

Doggy Day Care Flood 2015

On May 26, 2015, You Lucky Dog, a small family-owned doggy day care and boarding center, fell victim to devastating floods that hit Houston. There was insurance on the building itself but not on the contents, because for the past thirty years, through the worst of Houston's floods, the most water that ever got into the building was a few inches.

In the early morning hours, the nearby Brays Bayou breached its banks and water started rising inside the You Lucky Dog building. There were twenty-three dogs boarding over the Memorial Day holiday. Betsy, the overnight pet care specialist, worked diligently through the night to move all the dogs from their doggy dens to crates in higher spots in the building to keep them safe. The water rose steadily through the night to two-and-a-half feet deep throughout the building, and when the power went out, Betsy found herself working in waist-deep water in the dark.

Charlotte Petrey, the business' owner, and Leona and Joe Fortner, the day care managers, were desperately trying to get to You Lucky Dog. Every road they tried was blocked by floodwater. After they had gotten as close as they could by car, Joe decided to walk. His three-mile journey took him almost three hours, and at times he waded through chest-high water to reach the dogs and Betsy.

Thankfully, due in large part to the heroic efforts of Betsy, all twenty-three dogs were saved, but the devastating effects of the flood became apparent as the waters receded. Play areas, furniture, grooming tables, desks, computers and office equipment, doggy bedding—essentially everything inside the building was ruined.

Charlotte and her Paws Team at You Lucky Dog care deeply for their dogs and treat each one as if they were their own. Most pet boarding facilities don't keep staff in place overnight but Charlotte always felt that someone was needed to ensure the safety of the pets in the event of an emergency. The importance of that overnight person was never as clearly demonstrated as it was the night of the flood. The animals' safety was the top priority of the You Lucky Dog staff, even before their own.

How Planning and Preparation Saved a Boarding Facility

Smart, resourceful thinking, planning and implementing saved lives that night, and now Charlotte shares her in-the-flooded-trenches experience and offers practical, real-world advice to help other facilities. Thanks to her prepared planning, she didn't lose the most important thing—lives—and she also gained much knowledge for future planning, essential knowledge she now shares with her pet care industry colleagues.

Keep Your Head on Straight and Your Information in the Cloud

Though the facility was a complete loss, most records were saved because they were stored in "the cloud" or via a weekly backup drive that was rotated off-site. Clientele information and vaccination records were still at the facility's fingertips and information was safe even after floodwaters claimed the computers. Moving forward, Charlotte says she is converting all remaining paper records to electronic files and will continue to save data weekly for safekeeping and store it on a portable "travel drive" or in the cloud.

A Trained, Overnight Staffer is Worth "Every Dime"

Until her business reopened, Charlotte referred out all of her clients, with many of them asking for one specific requirement of the new facility: a trained overnight staffer. Charlotte started a revolution in the pet industry, an industry that needs more out-of-the-box thinkers like Charlotte, who confirms that "every dime invested (in an overnight staffer) paid off that night." She also advises making sure to keep open lines of communication with your overnight staff.

"Have a routine," she says, "so you know if something is up."

Charlotte advises not only knowing your staff and their capabilities, but also drilling down to the practical details, like investing in portable cell phone chargers that do not require an electrical outlet.

For her post-flood rebuild, in addition to investing in kennels that have access to a permanent lifted kennel platform that is easily accessible and allows the staff to provide a safe place for the dogs should water ever enter her facility again, Charlotte also installed a loft bed to give the employee a safe place to go.

Get Off the Insurance Fence

Charlotte encourages anyone riding the fence on flood and/or fire insurance to get off the fence and "do it right away."

One of many things Charlotte learned from this flood is the importance of covering her contents in her flood insurance policy, something she had not done.

"Without insurance, FEMA does not assist with small business disaster relief," she notes. "Know your limits on damages and look into disaster relief preparedness."

Reach Out and Communicate

Charlotte stresses the importance of not only implementing a means to manage and communicate with the owners of the pets you are housing during a disaster but also getting to know your local Red Cross, Humane Society and other disaster relief personnel. If possible, have them out to your facility to train.

"Know your outlets before you need them," Charlotte advises. "In case you ever have to reach out to them, you already have a foothold in the door."

But she also warns to not make them the totality of your preparedness plan. Although they were prepared for inches of water, virtually no one was prepared for the over thirty inches of water and historic flooding, causing even the Humane Society difficulty in reaching the facility. By the time they were close enough to put boats in the water to rescue the dogs, the waters had started to recede.

"It would have been too late if we had solely relied upon their efforts," Charlotte recalls. "Quick thinking and planning saved those dogs and our staff."

Invest in Preparedness Training ... Today

"Back up your computers, plan for flooding, plan for fire, plan through training, plan, plan, plan."

Charlotte cannot stress enough the importance of planning. She speaks from experience when she emphasizes that while an emergency plan will cost you financially now, it will save you so much more in the future, and may even save your business.

"We lost everything material, but we could have lost so much more," Charlotte notes.

"Share My Story"

Charlotte knows that her "loyal, dedicated, trustworthy" staff risked their lives to save the dogs and each other and, "in the scheme of things knew what to do, used their training to work through the situation." Nevertheless, she says, while they were prepared and had a plan, they "could have done much more" and have "learned much."

Ultimately, Charlotte says, "I want you to share my story, and educate other pet industry facility owners, managers, and supervisors that training is essential, planning is of utmost importance, and though we were never fully prepared, we saved those dogs, and that was important."

You Lucky Dog reopened for business on July 27, 2015.

Author photo

REAL LIFE STORY

Susan Briggs is a former owner and manager of Urban Tails, a full service pet resort in Houston, Texas. After twelve productive years in hands-on pet care, she is now a consultant for the pet care industry through her own company, Crystal Canine, and in partnership with Robin Bennett as The Dog Gurus.

Urban Tails' Experience With Natural Disaster

Would anyone anticipate that in twelve years of operating a business they would experience three different natural disasters? In hindsight this may have been a message from the universe, but I can honestly say each experience held an important lesson that it's an honor to share with you.

Urban Tails opened its doors in December 2000 as the first cage-free sleepover dog day care in the city of Houston. We were pioneers in the day care and cage-free boarding industry and we were figuring out processes as we grew. In those days we had to explain to prospective clients the benefits of day care and why they would pay for their dog to attend.

Three partners opened Urban Tails, as we knew the overnight schedule would be grueling. Between us we covered all dog day care day shifts, reception, overnights and all other business duties. So when we hired our first two full-time staff members in May 2001 we were very excited to have help.

By early June, our new staff were trained and we scheduled Don to cover the first overnight shift without an owner. Things looked good when we left that Friday evening in the rain. The three partners were so excited to all be going home to our own beds. It was a milestone for our business and a relief to the ownership team.

Around two in the morning my phone rang and it was Frances, one of my partners, on the line. Don had called and there was at least six inches of water in the building. The rain that night from Tropical Storm Allison was more than the city could take after 15 days of the storm lingering in the area. Parts of the city near our business had gotten more than twenty inches of rain in twenty-four hours. There was water in homes and businesses in areas of the city that had never flooded before.

Since I live pretty close to Urban Tails and I drive a truck, my initial reaction was *I'll just go down there and help Don.* When I went outside and saw the street in front of my house flowing like a creek, with a big log floating by, I realized that was not going to happen.

Don had secured the five dogs that were boarding with us that night in our cat condos. Yes, everything in Texas is bigger and our cat condos were multi-level 3′×4′×6′ units that sat on top of 2′ storage cabinets. So Brody, the Australian shepherd, and Chef, the Weimaraner, remained comfortable, high and dry. Frances stayed in contact with Don and the partners throughout the night and next morning. During the wait, Don worked in the building to raise key equipment and supplies above the rising water.

By mid-morning the rain had stopped and we all found routes to the business. The water had peaked at eighteen inches in the building and the task before us was cleaning up 20,000 square feet of business and warehouse space. In those days we used dog litter in our day care potty areas and sold pet kibble. A flood factoid is that both of these items swell and float everywhere!

The cleanup task was overwhelming, but adrenaline kicks in and the need to keep your business viable drives you. We did not have flood insurance so we knew that funding the cleanup was up to us, and our initial goal was to minimize the number of days we were closed without revenue.

We contacted clients to let them know their dogs were safe and took the boarders into our own homes for the remainder of their stays. We knew that our groom area was a small space, easier to clean and get operational quickly. We could also operate day care in our outdoor play yards once the reception area and building leading to the yards was clean and safe for dogs.

So five days after the flood we opened our groom shop and three days later our day care. We were still doing a lot of cleaning and disinfecting in our building as all walls had to be physically wiped down to prevent mold growth. We also had to remove our rubber mat flooring in our playrooms so the subfloor could dry. This was very physical work, as each mat weighed 100 pounds and had to be individually cleaned of mud and disinfected. Then 5,000 square feet of rubber flooring was reinstalled and seams caulked.

Through this experience I formed a love for the pet care industry and knew this would be my life's work. Of course, our family and friends helped us do the work to reopen Urban Tails, but we were also overwhelmed by the number of clients that came and helped. We also heard from vendors that replaced much of our destroyed inventory for free or at a discounted price.

Operating without any kind of a disaster plan, we did well at creating one as we moved through the experience. After Allison, we did purchase flood insurance and ensured that our computer equipment was kept at least one foot above the floor.

My biggest takeaway is that disasters happen quickly and without warning. No one is immune, so investing time creating a plan is a responsibility we accept when we open a service taking care of other people's pets. The physical aspect of the building was easy to repair, and most importantly the dogs in our care were safe. Our decision to staff our center 24–7 saved lives and allowed us to recover and become a stronger business. We learned trust in our staff, as Don did a terrific job without any type of disaster plan or training on our part. We also learned that opening a small business means you join communities locally and within the industry that will support you.

The interesting thing about disasters is that they can come in many different forms. After Tropical Storm Allison (the only non-hurricane to have the name retired), we created hurricane disaster planning for our center. Our second experience came in late August, 2005, when Hurricane Katrina caused the evacuation of New Orleans.

Since we were out of the hurricane landfall cone, we did not anticipate any involvement in this storm. However, as the storm moved closer and the damage grew, our phones started ringing. Many of the residents of New Orleans were heading to Houston for safety and needed a place to board their pets.

This took us by surprise and we saw a great opportunity to help people and their pets. However, we learned immediately that we needed to make a decision about our policy requiring proof of vaccinations. The majority of people calling were already en route to Houston and in the best-case scenario, their pet had a rabies tag. But their local veterinarian offices were closed, and the majority of owners did not have paperwork providing evidence of vaccinations.

We assessed the risk of the situation for the pets and our business. We discussed the problem with other pet center owners in the city and we all agreed the need to help the pets and people of New Orleans was more important than paper proof of vaccinations, so we worked on the honor system.

Being staffed around the clock was a blessing in this disaster, as a drive that normally took five hours turned into ten or more for the people headed to Houston. Our phones continued to ring with updates on arrival times and more requests for lodging. We put our best customer service foot forward and accommodated the schedules of the evacuees and took arrivals throughout the night.

No one anticipated the devastation that Hurricane Katrina brought to New Orleans. We now felt a part of the story and had many "temporary guests" that had no idea when or if they could go back home. As business owners we wanted to help, but financially our business was not in a position to offer free boarding services to all the pets in our care. We did not charge for multiple pets sharing an enclosure and offered a small discount for single pets. We also provided activities at no charge and encouraged owners to come visit their pets and take them on outings.

Our primary takeaway from Katrina was the power of community and service to make a disaster as easy as possible for those directly affected. The gratitude and humor of those temporary clients in the face of losing their homes and possessions reinforced the importance of family safety and service. We also updated our disaster policy to incorporate joining a support network for other coastal communities. Additionally, we located pet centers in central Texas that could serve as evacuation centers for Urban Tails in the event a Category 4 or 5 hurricane targeted Galveston/Houston.

Three years later, that planning was tested when Hurricane Ike set a path of landfall near Galveston. The storm was forecast as a Category 3 so our disaster plan was to remain in our building due to its sound concrete block construction. We had a generator and a disaster plan we put into action. Our goal was to board as few pets as possible during the actual storm landfall. After Allison and Katrina we had been contacted by local hospitals and news organizations looking for a pet center to care for pets of their employees who work during a natural disaster. We agreed to serve in this role to support our community and felt that family pets should stay with their families if at all possible during a natural disaster.

A key part of our disaster plans was knowing in advance how many staff members we could count on to work prior to and during a storm. Your staff members have families that are their own priority when a disaster strikes your community. We had a roster of the staff members who would help us prepare the day before a storm and who would commit to working to care for pets during the storm. Our building was large so the plan was to convert our office and training rooms into family living quarters. Two owners and two employee families moved into Urban Tails to ride out Hurricane Ike and care for 50 pets that were boarding with us.

Ike passed through Houston in the early hours of the morning and we did lose power. Our generator powered our emergency LED light strands and fans that kept air moving. What we did not anticipate was how slippery our sealed concrete floors got without the HVAC operating. Trying to walk a dog to our potty areas felt like ice-skating, so we had to stop our normal procedures to address the personal safety risk.

We observed that the dogs we had taken to the potty areas were actually stressed to the point very few did eliminate. For everyone's safety and comfort we made the decision to not continue with potty walks. We fed the pets and spent time with them to provide comfort and stress reduction. Urban Tails always used holistic tools in the care of pets so our supplies of rescue remedy and lavender spray were very valuable.

Fortunately our power was restored by mid-morning and we were able to resume normal dog care procedures. However, we learned quickly that having four people care for 50 pets was more than a full-time job and exhausting in the stress of a disaster. We did have a family member that was not trained in pet care serve as our cook and handle all phone calls.

Hurricane Ike caused a lot of damage in Houston, with power lost in many neighborhoods including mine. My family lived at Urban Tails for a week while we waited for power to be restored. A big lesson learned was that gas pumps cannot operate without power, so even though we had a generator and supply of fuel, restocking was a challenge.

After Ike, my perspective changed. I decided that personal safety and well-being are far more important than business. Serving your community during a disaster must be balanced with the personal family needs of you and your employees.

Pets are members of our families and belong with us during a disaster. This was a lesson our nation learned from Katrina. After Ike we changed our hurricane policy to plan on closing if a storm was predicted at Category 3 or above (previously it was 4 or 5).

Pet care is a service business and requires people to ensure quality care. We're responsible for ensuring a safe work environment for our teams. I've also learned through three disasters that each one is unique and will definitely provide new lessons.

Disaster planning is a necessity for every business, but especially pet services where we are responsible for the lives of precious family members. Know your team and their personal situations before a disaster strikes your community. Be conservative in your estimate of your abilities to continue operating your business in service to your community during a disaster, as the unexpected does happen.

Don't count on using normal operating procedures or staffing. As a pet care provider, the one situation I never wanted to experience was calling a client to advise them a pet had died in my care. This is the guiding principle we used each time we learned lessons and revised our plans to be more conservative. It's one I hope you will use as you create or revise your own disaster plans.

Loss of Utility Service or Power Outage

> TRY LIVING THROUGH ONE WEEKEND AT HOME WITHOUT ELECTRICITY, HEAT (INCLUDING HOT WATER), PHONE, OR THE USE OF YOUR CAR, AND YOU WILL QUICKLY GET THE IDEA OF HOW THIN A LINE EXISTS BETWEEN MODERN SOCIETY AND THE STONE AGE. (MICHAEL SEESE, 2010)

While most businesses could survive short-term without utilities, it certainly isn't a pleasant prospect. Many of the transactions of your business depend on electricity. Your interactions with prospective customers depend on the phone lines working. If you sell frozen pet food, your freezers hold thousands of dollars' worth of inventory.

Loss of utilities could mean that you lose your phone or Internet connections or that there is no warm water for baths because the natural gas line got shut off. If your building runs entirely on electricity, you may have to close for the duration.

Mitigation and Prevention for Loss of Utilities

- Buy a portable generator or install a permanent generator that will run critical appliances
- If you lease your facility, obtain landlord permission to install or use a generator
- Consider heating or cooling only a part of your facility during a power outage
- Identify alternate locations for animals that will be adversely affected by heat or cold
- Purchase business interruption insurance that has no waiting period and covers loss of utility events
- Pet sitters should have a plan for getting clients' animals relocated if necessary
- Secure an alternate source of water
- Do not use candles or other sources of open flame around animals
- Drive carefully; citywide power outages often mean that traffic lights are not functioning

HEADLINES

Pet Shop Owner Gets Creative After Power Outage

A pet store owner was in danger of losing all of the animals in his store due to an ice storm that caused area-wide power loss for over fifteen hours. The store owner used a fish fryer to boil water and heat water bottles to warm the water in his aquariums. Some of the other animals were put into the owner's car for warmth. Other birds had their cages wrapped in blankets with heated bottles placed in the bottom. After this episode, the owner purchased an indoor propane heater.

Pet Shop Becomes Refuge for Family Pets During Long Power Outage

A lengthy power outage forced many people into warming centers. They had no place to take their pets, so a pet store that did not lose power became a boarding center for exotic animals. Birds, fish, rodents and reptiles were taken in by the store.

Temperature Extremes

Take precautions during both summer and winter that will keep your staff more comfortable and able to take proper care of the animals in your facility. Extreme temperatures, whether ice- or heat-related, can be life-threatening, especially for very old or very young dogs and cats. Birds and exotic animals are sensitive to temperature changes and should be closely monitored.

CanStockPhoto

Mitigation for Temperature Extremes

- Adjust your hours so that your customers can get through ice or snow to get to your business
- Communicate with your customers via email or social media to let them know what is happening with your facility

- Consider using Skype or other face-to-face computer communication methods for consultations
- If business is slow or you are forced to close, use employee time creatively by having staff work on catch-up or reorganizing projects
- Keep animals indoors during extreme temperatures to avoid hypo- or hyperthermia
- Consider transferring hospitalized or special needs animals to a facility that still has power
- Keep fans and safe portable heaters on hand to keep employees and pets comfortable
- Keep your vehicle in weather-safe condition to prevent missing pet sits
- Have emergency contact numbers available so that clients' pets will be cared for if you cannot make it to a pet sit
- Use extreme caution when driving to appointments in icy weather
- Keep a seasonally appropriate emergency kit in your vehicle at all times
- Make sure that employees and animals are properly hydrated
- Dress appropriately for the weather

HEADLINES

Keeping the Doors Open During Bad Weather

A major ice storm left seventy percent of a city, including an animal clinic and pet resort, without power for eight days. The pet resort generally boarded sixty dogs; instead, during the period after the ice storm, the facility housed 167 dogs.

The facility was able to stay open because the veterinarian who owned the practice kept generators and propane heaters on hand for emergencies. Staff members who could make it to work carried flashlights and kept manual records until the computers were working again two days after the ice storm hit.

Pet Business Trying to Keep Animals Cool without Power

Storms across the eastern United States left thousands of homes without power during the extreme heat of the summer. A boarding facility was caring for more than one hundred pets when the power outage occurred. Staff members did everything that they could to keep the pets cool, including spraying the siding on the building with water to reduce the temperature inside the building.

Vehicle Maintenance Is a Critical Part of an Emergency Plan

Keep your vehicle in the best shape possible at all times:

- Change oil and other fluids regularly
- Keep tires in road worthy condition (including the spare); have snow tires or chains available if necessary in your area
- Keep your vehicle's fuel tank at least half full

Keep a vehicle safety kit in your car that includes:

- Booster cables
- Flashlight with extra batteries
- Lifehammer (tool that can break windshields and cut seatbelts)
- Windshield scraper
- Kitty litter or sand
- Area maps
- Water

Pandemic

A pandemic is a disease outbreak over a large geographic area that affects a large section of the population. Most diseases that caused such outbreaks are now considered eradicated, due to antibiotics and other medical care.

Influenza is caused by a virus and is not susceptible to antibiotics. Because of this, there is nothing that can be done to cure the disease. Influenza costs U.S. businesses over $30 billion per year. The influenza virus mutates readily and can affect humans as well as animals. Some scientists have predicted that the next influenza outbreak will affect millions worldwide.

In recent years, there have been two strains of canine influenza making the rounds. The initial strain identified, H3N8, has caused the illness of thousands of dogs across the United States. Kennels and other related businesses in several cities were forced to close due to canine influenza, some permanently.

The panic related to the outbreak of the second strain of canine influenza, H3N2, began early in 2015 and caused many kennels, groomers and day care facilities to require that all dogs receive the canine influenza vaccine. However, the only available vaccine at the time was for H3N8, and that vaccine was not effective against the H3N2 strain. Vaccines for the H3N2 canine influenza were not approved by the U.S. Department of Agriculture until the end of 2015.

A pandemic that could affect your pet care business might not be flu-related. In 1993, there was a cryptosporidium outbreak in Milwaukee when one of the city's two water treatment plants became contaminated. About 403,000 people in the area became ill (later studies have stated that this was a low estimate of the infection's spread). Although cryptosporidiosis is usually uncommon in dogs and cats, many animals carried the protozoa and were able to transfer the disease to humans and other animals. This was the largest waterborne outbreak in United States history. The cause of the contamination was never found.

Mitigation and Prevention for Pandemics

- Ensure that a backflow prevention device has been installed at your facility to prevent bacteria and other contaminants from entering the potable water supply
- Stockpile items such as soap, tissue, hand sanitizer and cleaning supplies; make sure that employees and customers have easy access
- Encourage employees to receive appropriate vaccinations (consider paying for the vaccinations if employees' health plans do not cover vaccinations)
- Encourage sick employees to stay at home
- Plan for employees that cannot report to work due to sick family members
- Cross-train employees to take over absent staff members' duties
- Have a contingency plan in place in case short-term boarding or day care becomes longer-term due to owner illness

HEADLINES

Pet Day Care Shuts Down After Parasite Outbreak

Three dogs contracted giardia, which caused a doggy day care and boarding kennel to close down so that the building could be disinfected. After the kennel reopened, another dog was diagnosed with the parasitic condition. The kennel's owner then decided to close the business permanently. The kennel had been open for fifteen years.

Dog Day Care Businesses Hit by Canine Flu

Several Chicago dog day care businesses were forced to close temporarily to prevent the spread of a contagious influenza virus that affected over a thousand dogs in the area. During the outbreak, pet owners were being advised to stay away from boarding and day care, grooming salons and dog parks.

HOW DO YOU PREPARE FOR THESE CRISES?

An industrial disaster could be caused by negligence, terrorism or by an act of nature. Crises can occur as follow-ons to the original disaster: rain storms may cause mudslides, or dogs may escape following a tornado that damages a kennel building.

Some crises are completely overlooked either because they "couldn't ever happen" or are so unusual as to be unthinkable. Accordingly, plans are not made, to the potential detriment of the business owner. It is impossible to plan for every contingency. Some disasters are so devastating that a business has little to no chance of recovery.

The best way that you can prepare for unforeseen circumstances is to make yourself fiscally ready and physically ready to the extent that you are able. With your "all hazards" crisis plan in place, you have a much better chance of staying open for business.

HEADLINES

Farmer Shoots Collies Dead After They Escape from Boarding Kennels While Owners Are on Holiday

While being boarded, two border collie mixes jumped a four-foot fence that separated the kennel's exercise field from a farmer's property. The kennel owner called for the dogs, and then went to find out whether the farmer had seen them. The farmer had shot both dogs point-blank as they crossed a brook on his property.

The farmer claimed that the dogs were worrying the sheep on the property. Law in the United Kingdom allows a dog to be shot for harming livestock. The authorities took no action against the farmer.

The kennel changed ownership and was renamed after this event.

On the Brink of Disaster—Again: Supervisor Seeks Help for Establishments That Survived the Quake Only to Face Failure Due to a Detour's Impact

After the Northridge earthquake, business owners whose buildings were unharmed thought that they had escaped a disaster. However, one road was turned into a bypass to keep the Golden State Freeway open, and that road happened to be the only access to several homes and businesses, including a long-established kennel facility.

Once the road became a bypass, clients could not safely turn into the kennel property, which cut off all income to the business. Suppliers and the post office stopped deliveries to the property. The kennel's owners were not eligible for emergency aid since they weren't considered direct victims of the earthquake. The detour remained in place until freeway reconstruction was completed. The owners lived off of their savings during that time.

The kennel owners overcame this crisis and closed in 2011 after forty years in business.

Man Sentenced in Doggy Day Care Heroin Case

The owner of a doggy day care was found guilty of dealing drugs from the business. The business was raided in 2014 and federal agents seized heroin, a large quantity of methamphetamine and "sizable amounts of cash." Drugs were hidden in a kennel, cash was buried under a dog house and a secret compartment held counterfeit twenty-dollar bills.

REAL LIFE STORY

Tony Clementi is a professional dog trainer in Illinois. He holds a master's degree in Education Curriculum and Development, and has worn many career hats: crisis planner, educator, dog day care owner and trainer.

My place, like many dog day cares, was located in a light industrial area. I had met with several of the other business owners in the area who had larger warehouse buildings. We'd made arrangements that if there was ever a fire or disaster that we could use their buildings as an evacuation point.

We had a series of events one summer. Our landlord worked on his classic car collection in the unit next to us. One day the alarm from our carbon monoxide detectors was set off due to the high levels of car exhaust drifting over from the landlord's unit. We had the ability to move all of our dogs to our outside play area and had evacuated our day care by the time the fire department arrived.

The fire department showed us that the carbon monoxide reading in our unit was almost twenty times higher than is safe. They placed large fans on both sides of the building and it took several hours for the building to clear out the fumes and reach normal levels. The initial high levels dropped quickly, but to fully flush out the building took two hours. Luckily it was a nice day and keeping the dogs outside wasn't an issue. If the temperature had been high heat or winter cold, we would have had to move the animals to another building and call clients to make early pickups. Our building did not have the ventilation for inside car work; in addition, classic cars produce fumes at higher levels than modern cars.

Unfortunately, this happened three more times. We mentioned the problems to our landlord, but nothing was ever resolved. After the fourth time in six weeks, we talked to the fire chief, who informed us that he had given the landlord previous warnings and that it had reached the point where he would begin to enforce fines. The problems then stopped.

We had plans for fire and disaster—even for gas leaks—but carbon monoxide wasn't even a thought.

PART FOUR: CRISIS RESPONSE

EVACUATE OR SHELTER-IN-PLACE

THE BEST WAY TO RESPOND TO A CRISIS IS TO BE PREPARED TO RESPOND BEFORE IT HAPPENS. YOUR BUSINESS CONTINUITY PLAN, DISASTER RECOVERY PLAN OR EMERGENCY RESPONSE PLAN IS DESIGNED TO HELP YOU PROVIDE A SAFE WORKING ENVIRONMENT. HOWEVER, IT IS UP TO EVERYONE TO ENSURE THE SAFETY OF THEMSELVES AND OTHERS. (DEBORAH C. MILLER, 2013)

CartoonStock/Mike Baldwin

The "all hazards" approach mentioned in the introduction to this book requires you to answer this question: "Should we stay, or should we go?" Although not every crisis will require you to respond in this way, all critical crises will require immediate action.

Many times you will know in advance of probable evacuation: weather events and wildfires are the most common reasons for evacuation. If you have advance notice that an evacuation is likely, do not wait for a mandatory evacuation notice. Start the evacuation protocol early; if evacuation turns out to be unnecessary, you can treat the situation as a practice drill. Follow through with a review of what worked and change the parts of the process that didn't go smoothly.

Fire, earthquake, or some other sudden disaster may require emergency evacuation of your premises. Your disaster binder will contain your evacuation protocol, maps for evacuation and critical contact information for employees, clients and service providers. Make sure that your plan is clear and detailed so that it can be implemented quickly.

Among other decisions that you will have to make is this critical one: will it be your business' policy for employees to attempt to evacuate animals, or will you require that employees wait for first responders to remove animals from the premises? Above all, keep your employees' safety in mind: whether or not they are evacuating animals, once they leave the building, they should remain outside and not try to reenter.

Always, always do a head count to make sure that all humans and animals are out of the building. At Cottonwood Animal Hospital in Ottawa, Kansas, the daily count of boarding pets is recorded by species on a white board hung just inside the boarding area. The white board is on the clinic's "grab" list so that employees can compare it to the post-evacuation head count.

Adequate shelter, protecting against both natural and man-made disasters, should be provided for employees when evacuation is not feasible. (ASIS International, 2003)

Instead of evacuation, shelter-in-place may be the strategy you must choose to stay safe. Chemical or biological contaminants may be released into the air. If these contaminants are harmful to people or animals, you will need to seal the doors, windows and vents in your predetermined shelter space. A bomb threat or unpredicted tornado could also cause a need to shelter-in-place. If you are advised to stay sheltered by civil or military authorities, do so.

Evacuation and shelter-in-place protocols are listed in Part Seven and in the Customizable Crisis Response Plan for Pet Care Businesses in the Appendix.

COMMUNICATION PLAN

When a disaster hits your business, there are a lot of people who will be interested: employees, clients and the public will need to know what happened and how you are going to make things normal again. No matter how long recovery takes, keep the status of your business up-to-date. People will feel that you are hiding something if for some reason you choose not to communicate.

Involve Clients in Disaster Response—Reverse 911

Consider asking your clients to be part of your response team:

- Include clients that would be willing and able to come to your aid in an emergency.
- Write a blanket message that will be used in a crisis and set up your phone or email to deliver the message on demand.
- When your clients receive this message, they respond as directed to help with evacuation or other tasks.
- The response team is authorized to take other clients' pets home with them if necessary and care for the animals until they can be retrieved by their owners.

Your first obligation is to your employees. Don't leave your employees uninformed or make them learn the latest news from the public or on social media. Your employees look to you for reassurance and leadership. They need to know whether to report to work, when to report to work and what your plan is for rebuilding. Use your employee contact tree for initial voice contact if phone lines are working.

After your employees, communicating with your clients is your next priority. An initial statement to your clients will be simple to send if you keep a current client database in both digital and hard copies.

Your clients are concerned with what happened, how you are dealing with the situation and when your business is likely to reopen. You will be more likely to elicit customer sympathy and maintain hard-earned customer loyalty if your business appears confident in the messages that you are sending and well prepared for any contingency. Continued client contact can be maintained through:

- Emails and text messages
- Social media—choose one or two platforms that most of your clients use
- A "dark website" that is already set up and can be activated in an emergency
- A hotline with regularly updated messages

All messages should be considered public, so make sure that your updates are carefully crafted. Some guidelines are:

- Become familiar with how to post news on social media outlets such as Facebook and Twitter. If you are not comfortable communicating through social media, then this is a task that an employee might be willing to assume. All messages should be approved before being posted.
- Build your social media audience before disaster strikes. People won't get your message if they don't know where to look.

- Refer all media inquiries to the company's designated representative so that messages are consistent.
- Stay focused on the message that you want to convey.
- If the incident is isolated to just your facility, most people will have less empathy, since it is likely that they were not affected. Frequent updates will keep your business in the public's eye.
- Your morale and that of your employees is important. Keep your messages as positive as possible without downplaying the event.

If you are caught up in a crisis that was caused by you or someone that you employ, chances are good that you will be attacked on social media or even through mainstream media. Negative posts, reviews and news pieces have a way of perpetuating themselves. You can overcome the negativity by accepting responsibility for the event without blaming others. If you cannot add to the available information, say so, or tell questioners that you will get back to them with the answers to their questions. Don't lie about the incident. Never lose your temper and write snarky replies. Above all, express genuine concern for those affected and then concentrate on doing what it takes to get your business through the crisis.

EMPLOYEES' ROLE IN A CRISIS

Events that affect your business affect your bottom line, and potentially the job security of your employees. You must have employee support during a response to any serious crisis; your business' survival depends on it. Throughout training and preparation exercises, emphasize the importance that you place on working together during a crisis. Be sure that each employee understands their role in the disaster response plan and their importance to the recovery of your business after a disaster.

When advance warning of a potential crisis is available, anyone with a health issue that could be made worse by the crisis should be released immediately. These employees can be kept busy by supporting your communication efforts, either from home or from an alternate location. Release other employees when their disaster plan duties have been completed. Once the premises are secure, all employees who are not staying on-site should be released with enough time to get to shelter.

Ensure staff welfare during and after a crisis event:

- Understand and respect each person's limitations
- Keep track of your staff's families; do they need something that you can provide?
    - Cash advances
    - Salary continuation
    - Flexible work hours
    - Family care packages
- Supply all of the items needed for employees to fulfill their disaster response and recovery duties
- Provide food and refreshments on a regular basis
- Frequent breaks are crucial to restore energy during the stress of a disaster situation
- Express your gratitude to those who are committed to aiding you in restoring your business functions
- Allow time for staff members to speak privately with a counselor if the need arises

Businesses that survive an adverse event often become stronger because of the extraordinary team effort that was required to respond to the emergency. Build your team with great care, train each employee in what is expected of them during a crisis and then support them as they work hard to protect and restore your company's assets.

A culture of planning and preparedness in the workplace is a large part of a successful business crisis plan. As you plan and train with your team, home preparedness should become part of the mix. Are your employees prepared to meet a disaster in their homes? An unprepared employee is not as valuable to your company as one who has prepared home and family for disaster and is therefore able to report to work.

> **If I truly believe that my calling in life is to be a steward to the animal population, then consistent with that stewardship is my earnest effort to prepare myself and my family such that I can leave them to provide that very necessary service and not feel as though I've left them in harm's way. (Dr. Jim Hamilton, VMAT 3 Founder and Commander, 2006)**

However, for the same reasons that few pet care businesses have emergency plans, few of your employees will prepare themselves and their families for disaster without encouragement. The resources for employee training in Part Eight include training on at-home preparation. Use the videos during staff training; they're each only a few minutes long and convey a lot of information. Provide incentives for preparation. We in the pet care industry know that positive reinforcement goes a long way in getting us the behaviors that we want!

PART FIVE: BUSINESS CONTINUITY AND RECOVERY

PHYSICAL AFTEREFFECTS

Returning from an evacuation or emerging from shelter in place has you holding your breath. What will you find: a few missing shingles, or your entire building in splinters? Have all of the people and animals in your circle come through the crisis uninjured? What comes next?

> The Small Business Development Center in your city has resources to help you. These centers are geared toward creating new jobs in the area but are happy to help small business owners in most situations. The business center will give you access to computers, fax machines, copiers and printers. Small business loans may be available that aren't tied to disaster or insurance status.

Your first steps should be to:

- Use your employee contact tree to get in touch with employees.
- Check on-site animals and staff (seek medical care if necessary).
- Initiate communication plan for clients.
- Notify outside agencies of status.
- Access critical contact list.
- Contact your insurance companies.
- Take a detailed inventory:
    - Pharmaceuticals, including vaccines
    - Controlled drugs (veterinarians must follow federal and state regulations and keep drug cabinet locked)
    - Surgical supplies
    - Pet food

    - Retail inventory

- Assess damage to facility, supplies, inventory and equipment.
- If repairs or cleanup are necessary:
    - Take extensive and detailed pictures before cleaning or repairing anything.
    - Make only mitigating repairs until you have sent a preliminary report to your insurance companies and cleanup has been approved.
    - Use protective gear during cleanup: gloves, long sleeves and pants, eye protection.
    - Clean and disinfect everything that you plan to reuse.
    - Do not turn on gas—a representative from the gas company should inspect pipes and connections.
    - Inspect and test all electronics at least twice to make sure that they are not damaged by smoke or dust.
    - Call an electrician to check the building before connecting any appliance or tool.
    - Have a plumber check water pipes if burst water pipes are a concern.
    - Obey "boil water" orders from officials. Do not use well water until the well has been tested. Do not use flood water for any purpose.

If you can keep at least part of your business going during the recovery phase, you will be able to mitigate your damages and keep your customers coming through the door. Being able to board animals while their owners are in shelters will ease your clients' minds. Opening your business so that people can purchase food for their pets means a lot.

> Having a contingency plan that puts equipment or staff to work in an alternative way can mitigate losses. (Gwendolyn Bounds, WSJ Online)

Some of your employees will have family obligations and will need to make those a priority; otherwise, you can keep your employees busy running the business, doing cleanup activities and helping with client communication. Once you have seen to your own needs, and if you have the manpower and resources to do so, reach out to colleagues, clients or rescue groups that may not have been as prepared to deal with the disaster as you were.

Survivor's Guilt

Often after a disaster strikes, people you know and complete strangers may show up at your doorstep wanting to help in some way. There could be multiple reasons for this outpouring of support, including:

- A willingness to help because they were not affected by the disaster
- Gratitude for services that you may have performed for them in the past
- General love for animals

Even though you may desperately need help, be wary of accepting strangers as volunteers. They are not familiar with your policies and procedures and may not be conditioned for the type of work that you need them to perform. They may not have completely honest intentions and you may find cash or controlled substances missing.

If people unknown to you ask to help, direct them to the centralized disaster center in your community. There will be a volunteer coordinator there that can assign each volunteer to work that suits his or her abilities and training.

EMOTIONAL AFTEREFFECTS

A major disaster is extremely stressful for both humans and animals, especially if the entire community has been affected or lives have been lost. Every person reacts differently; some recover more quickly than others. Some indicators that stress has become overwhelming are:

- Behavioral changes
- Fear and anxiety
- Lack of appetite
- Sleep disturbances

How quickly an individual recovers emotionally from a disaster situation depends mainly upon the disaster's level of disruptiveness in their life and the support system that they can count on. Sometimes, a person will not show any outward sign of psychological distress and then fall apart at the news of a distant event or on the anniversary of their own disaster. Others show emotional distress from the beginning; frequent crying or mood swings, confusion, indecisiveness and withdrawal are all signs that a person is having trouble coping with the current situation.

All of these responses are completely normal and may last for days or weeks. People are resilient and most are able to overcome adversity and adapt in time. It is common to suffer from distress in the immediate aftermath of a serious crisis. Some longer-term signs of distress include:

- Hypervigilance
- Depression
- Nightmares
- Recurring headaches
- Sudden bouts of anger

While it is important for routines eventually to return to normal, try to keep everything low-key immediately post-disaster. Eat small, frequent meals. Build a lot of rest time into your schedule. Children and animals will need reassurance and extra emotional support. If possible, mealtimes and bedtime should return to before-disaster patterns for children and adults. Other suggestions to move past thinking in "crisis mode":

- Give yourself time to adjust to the new normal.
- Talk about your feelings with others who experienced the same event and will empathize with you.
- Make time to get away from the disaster environment in order to get in touch with your thoughts on other things.
- Exercise and eat well.
- Avoid major life changes.

Watch for signs of distress in your employees, your family and yourself. The American Psychological Association recommends seeking help from a professional therapist if the symptoms of distress last for longer than a month after the disaster. Depending on the state in which you live, your workers' compensation insurance policy may cover this expense for your staff.

FINANCIAL AFTEREFFECTS

The disaster that hit your business left your animals and employees unscathed. Unfortunately, the building that houses your business was damaged. You have just overcome one challenge to be faced with another. The long-term survival of your business now depends on a successful trek through the claims process.

Call your insurance companies right away. You have contact information and copies of your policies in your disaster binder. Follow up with letters of notification the same day, noting the name of the company representative you spoke with and the basic details of the event. Confirmation letters can be sent either through email or with a proof of delivery, but it is important that you "date stamp" your initial contact in case there is a conflict with your insurance companies regarding notification.

Pay close attention to the sections of your policies that are titled "Duties After a Loss." This section will explain what you must do in order to get your claim paid. The most important responsibilities that you have are to (1) notify your insurance companies within a set time limit (which varies by policy and rider, so read carefully), (2) file a preliminary report of damages, (3) take action to mitigate further damages and (4) file a final report according to the insurance companies' requirements.

Document all expenses that you must pay to get your business running:

- Overtime wages
- Equipment purchased or rented
- Extra travel expenses for employees
- Meals purchased for employees
- Supplies purchased to facilitate cleanup
- Services contracted to mitigate or prevent further damages
- Fees for expert inspections

Train your employees to keep track of expenses: if in doubt, keep the receipt. You may be able to deduct expenses from your tax return that your insurance did not reimburse.

> **THE GENERAL RULE OF THUMB IS TO CALL ONLY WHEN YOU ARE SURE THAT THERE HAS BEEN AROUND TWO TO THREE TIMES THE AMOUNT OF THE DEDUCTIBLE PROPERTY DAMAGE DONE. (ROBERT WINTER, 2015)**

Write up your preliminary insurance claims reports. Make a report for each insurance company, keeping in mind that some coverage could overlap. Include date, time, nature of the damages and claim number (if you were assigned a number during your initial contact). Provide your contact information and let your insurance companies know whether you have taken action to mitigate further damage. Keep track of any changes or additions to these preliminary reports.

Check your premises from roof to basement and all of the contents. Verify that all of the mechanicals are in working order even if there is no apparent damage (hire experts if necessary). After your utilities are restored, plug in appliances one by one. Double check that computer equipment and other electronics are not clogged by dust or smoke. Make a written list of the damage that you find. Back up your written list with photographs. Pictures should be taken of damage before and after you make mitigating repairs. If you have not documented a loss, then an insurance company's adjuster will assume that there was no loss.

If you have multiple policies, you will have to deal with multiple claims adjusters. If you have been injured or are overwhelmed by the scope of the crisis, now is the time to consider hiring a professional public insurance adjuster. A public insurance adjuster works for a percentage of your paid claim and works exclusively in your best interest. They can provide help with inventories and claims and can even represent you with your insurance companies to get you the best possible payout on your policies.

If you choose not to hire a public insurance adjuster, you will meet with each adjuster and provide your written and photographic inventories. (Pre-disaster inventories are in your disaster binder.) Mark each item that you provide to the adjusters with your contact information and claim number. Make sure that each adjuster you meet has your contact information in case there are questions. Ask the adjuster to provide you with a list of requirements for a final report, if one is available.

You will use your written and photographic evidence again when preparing your final reports for the insurance companies. Organize each report according to the specific instructions provided by each policy in order to get your claim addressed quickly. Include evidence of lost revenues (profit and loss statements, tax records) and documentation of mitigation expenses.

If you have a financial cushion and can afford to do so, starting cleanup and repair can get you on the road to recovery and get customers back into your business. Read your policies carefully to make sure that there isn't a prohibition on starting reconstruction. Some insurance companies require that you use contractors that are on their approved list. You could endanger your claim payment if you don't follow the policy language to the letter.

Hairy Situations

Several scenarios might come up during the claims payment process:

- You might be offered less money than you are entitled to in order to get your claim processed quickly.
- You could be offered a partial payout of what you think you're entitled to. Be careful. Some companies will include language on the check that prohibits you from further claims and you agree if you endorse the check. Reputable companies do not do this.
- The settlement that is offered may be less than what you think you should be getting. If this happens, you don't have to accept the first offer. Go back over your policies and speak with the adjusters again. Check the payout offer against the language of the policies.
- If you face an unresolvable dispute with your insurance company over their offered settlement and you are sure that your claim is valid, you can report the company to your state's insurance commissioner or bring a lawsuit against the company for "bad faith."

Even after your claim has been settled, stay vigilant. There may be other damages that become apparent later. Know your policies' time limits on making further claims.

Wikimedia/FEMA/Greg Henshall

Register with FEMA (Federal Emergency Management Agency) if your business has been affected by a community-wide disaster (and your location is included in the declared disaster area). This is the first step to gaining access to funds that might be able to help your business recover. Relief for your small business and your employees can also come from the following agencies:

- American Red Cross—provides immediate help to individuals and small businesses that are registered as sole proprietorships
- Small Business Administration—disaster assistance loans, economic injury loans, military reservist economic injury disaster loans
- Internal Revenue Service—tax relief assistance
- Department of Labor—disaster unemployment assistance (available to small business owners as well as employees), flood recovery assistance

Disaster relief programs have different eligibility requirements and separate documentation is necessary to apply for each. The results can be extremely disappointing, given the amount of time and trouble that it takes to prepare the applications. Weigh your options carefully: there are going to be a lot of demands on your time and attention after a disaster. Your own efforts at crisis prevention and mitigation are likely to pay off far more favorably than any government program.

PART SIX: CONCLUSION

THERE IS A GROWING APPRECIATION FOR THE BENEFITS OF PREPAREDNESS. (FEMA, 2011)

Pet care businesses have a unique obligation in disaster planning and crisis preparation. Your clients have entrusted you with the safety and well-being of something precious to them. While you do not have control over how a disaster happens, you do have control over how you prepare for and protect against disaster. You cannot save lives if you do not respond confidently and quickly to any crisis that presents itself. Being able to respond instantly to any emergency is crucial to business continuity in the pet care industry.

Consider your planning and preparation efforts a work in progress. Continual training and practice are key components of your response plan. Engage your employees in activities that will cement their commitment to a culture of crisis prevention in your business. Work with your team to make your plan better after each practice drill.

Planning, preparing, testing and training takes time, it's true. However, the time spent in these activities is time well-spent. Everyone concerned will be grateful when a crisis affects your business and stress, frustration and downtime are minimized because you took the time to be ready. Being able to concentrate on the well-being of your family and your business in the aftermath of a disaster will speed and smooth the recovery process.

The use of an "all hazards approach" simplifies the planning process. Whether you need to evacuate or shelter-in-place, your business will be supported by the items in your disaster binder and facility disaster kit. Your team will be able to concentrate on what is most important: keeping your business viable and the animals in your care safe.

Time and again this book has shown that the benefits of crisis planning outweigh the costs. You have read stories of pet care business owners who were prepared to meet a crisis head-on, and others who didn't fare well because of poor planning or complete lack of planning. You now have the information and tools that you need to write a crisis plan for your business and prepare yourself so that you are able to keep your business going if disaster strikes. Use these tools to make your business disaster-resistant.

Plan to stay in business!

Once you have completed your business' crisis plan, use the fact that your business has planned and prepared for all hazards as a marketing tool. Feature your business' preparedness and training efforts on your website. Let your clients know that their animals are in well-prepared (and well-trained) hands.

- Host a pet safety event to communicate with the public about your plan
- Raise money to supply the local fire department with animal oxygen masks
- Stock branded pet first aid kits for purchase
- Invite first responders to hand out materials
- Provide home disaster preparedness checklists
- Host a pet first aid and emergency response class
- Invite your state's animal response team to share demonstrations or video

Be sure that the media is invited to your event—you and your team worked hard on your plan, and you deserve the attention!

PART SEVEN: PREPARATION, RESPONSE AND RECOVERY TOOLS

CUSTOMIZABLE CRISIS RESPONSE PLAN FOR PET CARE BUSINESSES

My mantra throughout writing this book has been, "Your response to a crisis is only as good as your plan." No plan means no coherent response. If you are procrastinating putting a plan together, start by copying the Customizable Crisis Response Plan pages from the Appendix, insert the pages into a binder, and fill out each section in pencil as you can. Make time in your schedule to do at least one section a week.

CanStockPhoto

Once you get started, you will think of items that are important to your business that you want to include in your binder, so make notes as you go. When you get all of the blanks filled in by hand, you will have a working plan. Pat yourself on the back—you have just done more crisis planning than more than 75 percent of small businesses ever complete.

When the "rough version" of your plan is completed, go to the *Hairy Situations* website (http://petbusinessdisasterresponse.com/crisis_plan/) to download the crisis planning forms. Make any changes to the format that you wish to make, insert the information that you have already written, and print out your business' crisis plan.

The key is to have all of the critical information that you need to keep your business running, or to get it back up and running quickly after a crisis. You want anyone who picks up your business' disaster binder to be able to find needed information within seconds. Time that you spend organizing your binder now will save time that you can't afford to lose during a crisis.

To complete your binders, you will need:

- Loose-leaf ring binders (at least three): Choose a color that will mean "CRISIS" in your mind. Do not use the same color binders for any other function in your business.
- Computer
- Printer (you will be making both color and black and white copies)
- Page protectors
- Page dividers
- CDs (one for each binder and one for each insurance adjuster, including a public adjuster if you hire one)
- CD holders for ring binders
- Flash drives (one for each binder)
- Pencil cases (two per binder)

- City map (draw on one and make copies to avoid repeating work)
- State map (again, just draw on one and make copies)
- Markers/pens
- Optional: label maker, business card holders for ring binders

You will make three or more binders at the same time: one for storage in a central (secure) location at your business, one for inclusion in your disaster kit, and one for an offsite location. If you make others, make sure that you note where they are stored and keep them updated.

The Customizable Crisis Response Plan for Pet Care Businesses includes the following:

1. Table of Contents
2. Binder Information
3. Communication Plan
4. Key Person Letters
5. Employee Contact Tree
6. Employee Skills/Cross-Training List
7. Critical Contacts List
8. Building Map (two copies for each binder)
9. Location of Hazardous Materials (two copies for each binder)
10. Site Map (two copies for each binder)
11. Area Map (two copies for each binder)
12. Localized Evacuation Checklist
13. Community Wide Evacuation Checklist
14. Evacuation Map (two copies for each binder)
15. Contact Information for Evacuation Destination (two copies for each binder)

16. Copies of Mutual Aid Agreements
17. Shelter-in-Place Checklist
18. Recovery Checklist
19. Emergency Policies and Procedures
20. Bank and Financial Information
21. Latest Profit and Loss Statements
22. Copy of Business Licenses, EIN Number and Sales Tax Permit
23. Copy of Legal Retainer
24. Insurance Information and Copies of all Insurance Policies
25. Copy of Lease or Mortgage Information
26. Written Inventory of Office Equipment and Furnishings (two copies in each binder)
27. Copies of Software Licenses/Installation Disks
28. Important Passwords and PINS
29. Hard Copies of Business-Related Forms
30. Binder Update Record

Pet sitters and trainers will need to adjust this plan to allow for unique situations. Pet sitters may need to plan for alternate caregivers for a clients' animals. Trainers may be boarding dogs in their own home and need to provide for them in the long term. The Emergency Policies and Procedures section is a good place to put your policies for these contingencies. This document can be written so that you can share it with your clients. You will also write your evacuation and shelter-in-place plans to fit your needs.

You might decide to carry a crisis plan binder in your company vehicle, or keep your binder in digital form. Your binder includes sensitive information, so be sure that you can keep it secure if you carry it with you.

All pictures and video that you have taken of the inside and outside of the building and all equipment should be put onto a CD and kept in a CD holder that you will include in your binder. Make one copy for each binder and one for each insurance adjuster that you will meet with during the recovery phase (including one for your public adjuster), plus one extra.

Do not put business documents on the same media (CD or flash drive) as your photos. You may not have the means to separate them later and you do not want to share your confidential information with anyone who is unauthorized to see it.

A Customizable Crisis Response Plan for Pet Care Businesses is included in the Appendix. Add or delete sections as necessary, input information, and then put a hard copy of the entire plan into each of your disaster binders. Update all of the binders on a regular schedule. The forms are also available in Word format on the *Hairy Situations* website (http://petbusinessdisasterresponse.com/crisis_plan/).

NOTE: Your completed crisis response plan should be considered a confidential business document and each binder should be kept in a secure place.

Evacuation Protocol

These checklists are written as general examples to get you started on your own list. Your circumstances are different, so you must adjust the checklists for your own needs. Add as much detail as necessary to make your procedure clear to your employees. Evacuation protocol charts for both localized and community-wide crises are included in the Customizable Crisis Response Plan for Pet Care Businesses document in the Appendix and online.

REMEMBER: Your evacuation list should be clear and detailed. Don't expect to rely on someone's memory in a stressful situation. Assign your employees duties so that each action step is covered.

Employees need to know:

- What to do
- What to grab
- Where to go

Localized Evacuation:

- Call 911 if alarm system has not automatically sent notification.
- Immediately release any employee whose health could be negatively affected by the crisis.
- Evacuate animals on leads or in Evacsacks and crate them once they are safely outside of the building.
- Move animals to a predetermined evacuation location (distance should be at least 300 feet from your facility).
- What to grab:
    - Disaster binder
    - Facility disaster kit
    - Identification
    - Keys
    - Date book/appointment calendar
    - Cell phone and charger
    - Laptop or tablet and power cords
    - Current controlled drug log (if you are evacuating from a veterinary clinic)
- Unplug equipment if time permits.
- Close all windows and doors (especially fire-rated doors) if time permits.
- Shut off electrical breakers, gas, and water (but DO NOT turn utilities back on without inspection by the utility company).
- Move vehicles to a predetermined safe location.
- Leave someone outside of your facility to communicate with first responders.

- Perform a head count of employees.
- Perform a head count of animals.
- Contact clients with your evacuation location and pickup procedures (you will have predetermined the method of communication with clients and it will be included in your disaster binder).
- Release remaining off-shift employees after all of the animals that have not been picked up have been moved to an alternate location.
- On-shift employees should report to the alternate location.

Community-Wide Evacuation:

- Listen to radio or television newscasts and follow the instructions given by the authorities.
- Load disaster kit into main vehicle in case evacuation notice is given.
- Contact pet owners and have as many pets collected as possible (you will have predetermined the method of communication with clients and it will be included in your crisis response plan).
- Bring loose objects into the facility to prevent them becoming hazardous in unstable weather conditions.
- Pre-assemble travel crates.
- Make sure that each vehicle that will be used in the evacuation is fueled and has an evacuation map.
- Load pets (in travel crates) into vehicles (if you are relocating exotics or birds, you must cool or heat vehicles prior to loading; their survival depends on it).
- Check all areas for hiders and keep a written head count as each animal is loaded.
- Release employees who have home commitments.

- What to grab:
    - ▫ Disaster binder
    - ▫ Identification
    - ▫ Keys
    - ▫ Date book/appointment calendar
    - ▫ Cell phone and charger
    - ▫ Laptop or tablet and power cords
    - ▫ Current controlled drug log (if you are evacuating from a veterinary clinic)
- Unplug equipment.
- Close all windows and doors (especially fire-rated doors).
- Shut off electrical breakers, gas, and water (but do not turn utilities back on without inspection by the utility company).
- Secure premises.
- Decide which evacuation route you will be taking.
- Post sign on door informing clients where you are heading and name of hotel or location of designated pet shelter, along with your cell number (premade copies are in your disaster binder).
- Release employees who will not be going to your evacuation destination.
- Contact alarm company.
- Contact evacuation location to let them know you are on your way.
- Contact all employees regularly to give status updates.
- Keep in contact with clients.

Shelter-in-Place Protocol

A Shelter-in-Place Protocol chart is included in the Customizable Crisis Response Plan for Pet Care Businesses in the Appendix and online.

The area of your facility that you use for shelter-in-place is important. If you can, choose an interior room that has direct access to a restroom. If an interior room is not available or there is not sufficient space to locate all of the animals in your care in an interior room, then designate a space that can be secured. The space that you use should be located away from any glass doors or windows and away from exterior walls if possible.

Remember that instructions to shelter in place are usually provided for durations of a few hours, not days or weeks.

- Keep track of the situation with a NOAA weather radio. Also listen to regular television or radio bands to hear the latest instructions for your area.
- Pre-assemble travel crates and move them into your safe room.
- Move your facility disaster kit to your safe room.
- Close the business and ask all clients and visitors to stay.
- What to grab:
  - ▫ Disaster binder
  - ▫ Identification
  - ▫ Keys
  - ▫ Date book/appointment calendar
  - ▫ Cell phone and charger
  - ▫ Laptop or tablet and power cords
  - ▫ Current controlled drug log (if your business is a veterinary clinic)

- Close and lock all windows and exterior doors.
- Shut off all vents, air-conditioning units and fans.
- Shut off air exchangers and air filters.
- Shut off all utilities if time permits.
- Bring all animals into the safe area and put them into travel crates; be sure to check for animals that may be hiding.
- Close and lock the door to the safe room.
- Seal off windows, doors and vents if there is a chance of contamination.
- Ask employees and others in the safe room to call their emergency contacts to let them know where they are and that they are safe.
- Change the message on your answering machine or messaging service to state your shelter-in-place status.
- Write down the names of all of the people and animals in the safe room and secure this list by taping it to the wall.
- Contact clients with your shelter-in-place information (you will have predetermined the method of communication with clients and the plan will be included in your disaster binder).
- Contact employees who are due to arrive for their shifts and advise them of your shelter-in-place status.
- Keep listening to the radio or television until you are told by authorities that it is safe to leave your shelter.
- Keep in touch with clients throughout the shelter-in-place period.

Facility Emergency First Aid Kit

Although "first aid" is meant to be used strictly as a preliminary to veterinary care, there may be instances in which you will find yourself caring for sick or injured animals without the ability to seek professional care for them. The list below is meant to help you prepare for such a situation.

If you are responsible for species other than cats or dogs, take the needs of those animals into account when creating the list of first aid items to be included in your own kit. Eliminate the items that are unnecessary for your business to have on hand. After you have adjusted this list according to your own needs (make a notation of the quantity of each item you plan to stock), ask a trusted veterinarian to go over the list with you. Ask the veterinarian to add to the list any items that she would consider necessary in an emergency situation, and ask her to explain the use of items with which you may not be familiar.

Each of your employees should be familiar with the location and organization of the facility emergency first aid kit, and should be trained in how to use each item on the list. Store the facility emergency first aid kit with the facility disaster kit. Just as with all of the other disaster supplies that you have stocked, it should be clearly marked EMERGENCY ONLY and not used for daily needs. Rotate perishable items on a regular basis.

Facility emergency first aid kit:

- Activated charcoal (effective in absorbing many toxins)
- Antibiotic eye ointment
- Antibiotic ointment (with pain reliever)
- Anti-diarrheal liquid or tablets
- Baking soda (good for soothing skin conditions)
- Bandage scissors
- Bandage tape
- Band-Aids (in case you forget your human kit)

- Benadryl
- Betadine or Nolvasan (to cleanse wounds)
- Bite gloves
- Blankets (foil emergency blankets)
- Clean cloths
- Cleansing agent (soap or antibiotic towelettes)
- Corn syrup (for diabetic dogs or those with low blood sugar)
- Cotton bandage rolls
- Cotton-tipped swabs
- Disposable gloves
- Elastic bandage rolls
- Gauze pads and rolls
- Grooming clippers or safety razors
- Hand sanitizer
- Hydrogen peroxide (to induce vomiting when directed by a veterinarian or poison control)
- Instant cold packs
- Isopropyl alcohol (to clean thermometer)
- Muzzle or strips of cloth to use for muzzling
- Needle-nosed pliers
- Non-adherent bandage pads
- Pedialyte
- Pediatric digital thermometer
- Penlight or flashlight

- Pet nail clippers
- Plastic syringes of various sizes (to administer medication orally)
- Sterile saline solution (for rinsing wounds and cleansing eyes of debris)
- Self-cling bandages
- Simethicone in liquid form (brand names include Gas-X and Maalox Gas)
- Slip leads
- Sterile lubricant (water-based)
- Styptic gel or powder (clotting agent)
- Tick scoop (for removing ticks or scraping out stingers)
- Towels
- Tweezers
- Ziploc bags in several sizes

Optional:

- Bloat kit
- Microchip reader
- Rescue Remedy flower essence (good for calming both pets and people)
- Veterinary skin stapler

The veterinarian that reviews this list with you should provide dosages for any over the counter medications that you have included in your kit. Do not rely on the internet to provide this information. Make sure that each package has a syringe attached if necessary and is labeled clearly with animal dosages.

Facility Disaster Kit

Constructing a facility disaster kit doesn't require a lot of time, trouble or expense. You can gather extra items that you may already have, or build a kit gradually by budgeting a certain amount per month to make purchases for the kit.

First, assess the space that you have to store your kit. Determine which items from the list are necessary for your business and gather items from the list, adjusting quantities according to your facility's needs. The last item on your purchasing list should be the containers that will hold your kit. They should be sturdy, somewhat weatherproof and modular for easy storage.

Flickr/CC/Alisha Vargas

The best way to organize your kit is by species and function. Packing three or more separate containers sounds like trouble, but when you are sorting through a box for one certain item, your pre-planning and organization will pay dividends by saving you time and aggravation.

Each staff member should maintain a supply of their own necessary personal emergency items at the facility.

Mark containers EMERGENCY ONLY. Place an inventory list in each container. Use the list to maintain inventory, expiration dates and to rotate food and water supplies as necessary.

Your facility disaster kit should be stored INSIDE your facility. Store the kit in a place that is high enough that the kit is unlikely to be affected by floodwaters. Some bulky items (such as travel crates or a generator) can be stored in an easily accessible outbuilding or shed.

Remember that pet products should be used only on the species named on the label. Take special care to monitor the well-being of very young, very old and very small animals.

Human supplies:

- Air mattresses or camping mats
- Blankets
- Cash (small bills)
- Change of clothes (seasonally appropriate)
- Chargers for cell phones, laptops, other devices
- Crisis plan binder
- Disposable dishes and flatware
- Extra set of keys
- First aid kit (use a basic purchased kit; many items from the animal kit can also be used on humans)
- Non-perishable food (plan for 2000 calories per day/per person)
- Personal hygiene items: toothbrushes, sanitary pads, moist towelettes
- Personal medications
- Towels

- Water—one gallon per person per day will serve for hydration and hygiene

Tools and supplies:

- Batteries (extras for each device; check and replace batteries regularly to ensure viability)
- Bleach—10 percent bleach as disinfectant/16 drops per gallon to purify drinking water
- Box opener
- Buckets (five gallon size) with lids (used for storage/sanitation)
- Bungee cords of various sizes
- Duct tape
- Dust masks/respirators that have been approved for use in hazardous situations by the National Institute for Occupational Safety and Health (NIOSH)
- Flashlights
- Garbage bags
- Generator
- Hand sanitizer
- Heavy gloves
- Ice chests (do not store kit supplies here)
- Light sticks (do not use candles; no open flames around animals)
- Local maps (multiple evacuation routes should be clearly marked)
- Manual can opener (or eliminate the need for this item by packing only pull top cans)
- Moist towelettes

- Multi-tool
- NOAA weather radio (battery powered/crank)—try to get a combination radio that will receive local frequencies
- Office supplies (pen, paper, permanent marker, tablet to document decisions and expenses)
- Old-style telephone that doesn't need electricity to work
- Paper towels
- Paracord
- Plastic bags (all sizes)
- Plastic sheeting
- Pocket knife
- Poncho for each employee
- Rubber or latex gloves
- Rubber boots to keep feet dry when working in flood waters
- Safety glasses/eye protection
- Sandbags
- Shovel (for filling sandbags)
- Scissors
- Tarp
- Toilet paper
- Two-way radios (in case of cell phone failure)
- Whistle (to signal for help)
- Wrench or pliers (to shut off utilities)
- Zip ties

Dogs, cats, other animals (separate kits for each species; some items will be duplicated between kits):

- Blankets
- Cat litter and portable litter pans
- Disposable dishes and flatware
- Evacsack or pillow cases (for cats)
- Facility emergency first aid kit (include medications for specific animals as necessary)
- Food (try to use dry or dehydrated food or pull top cans)
- Leashes and collars
- Misters, fans and heating pads (if needed for exotic pets and birds)
- Muzzles
- Slip leads
- Spray bottles
- Stainless steel water dishes
- Towels
- Treats and chews
- Toys
- Poop pickup bags
- Travel crates (one for every animal in your facility)
- Tags with facility name/contact information (place on the cages of small mammals and birds)
- Water

Employee Contact Tree

An employee contact tree serves several purposes: the information allows you to directly notify your employees of a critical incident, its use verifies the safety and well-being of your employees in a community-wide event and it helps you to determine which of your employees will be available to report to work. Without this list, you can count on working alone.

When contact is made with an employee, ask these questions:

- Are you and your family OK?
- Has your home been affected?
- Do you need anything that we can provide?

When designated callers have made contact with each employee on their call list, they should notify the first-tier caller with a report on what each employee's needs are and whether they will be able to report for work.

If you design your own call tree, try to keep the number of contacts that each person has to make to three or fewer. Keeping the contact requirements minimal will allow for multiple attempts to contact each employee as well as accommodate replies to messages and confirmation of availability.

The book's website (http://petbusinessdisasterresponse.com/crisis_plan/) has an employee contact tree file in Word format and an example is included in the Appendix. Add or delete levels as necessary, input contact information, and then put a hard copy of the list into each of your disaster binders. Update the list regularly.

A copy of the contact tree should be supplied to each employee so that contact can be initiated by anyone on the primary or secondary tier of the list. The list should be considered confidential.

Critical Contacts List

A comprehensive critical contacts list can make or break your business during the response and recovery phases of a disaster. Payment of insurance funds may depend on how quickly you contact your insurance company and file a preliminary claim, and yet contact information for your agent may be inaccessible if you have been forced to evacuate your building. During a crisis, you will have more important things to do than search for contact information.

During a community-wide event, calls to 911 may go unanswered due to overwhelming call volume or even the destruction of the system itself. If you need a first responder, having an alternate number to call can mean the difference between life and death.

It is important that you establish meaningful relationships with these critical contacts before you need them so that you are not making a cold call when you need help. In the case of service providers, make sure that you steer business their way, either through your own business or recommendations, so that they know you. Business people are more likely to place their best clients at the top of the list when the calls for help start to arrive.

Peers and colleagues in the pet care industry should definitely be included on this list. If you are a pet sitter, do you know a kennel operator that may be able to provide space for your animals? If you are a kennel, do you know of a pet store that will let you have crates or other supplies on credit? If you are a pet store, would a dog day care be willing to let you "borrow" some of their employees to help relocate animals if necessary? Remember, though, that these relationships are meant to be pre-established and reciprocal; don't ask for help out of the blue, and don't request aid if you wouldn't be willing to contribute goods or services in time of need.

Having this contact information in one document and included in your crisis plan may help in another way as well. In the event you are incapacitated or unable to reach your business during a disaster, any authorized employee with access to the list can start to make contact with the necessary vendors.

A critical contact list is included in the Appendix and on the *Hairy Situations* website (http://petbusinessdisasterresponse.com/crisis_plan/) in Word format.

Add or delete contacts as necessary, input contact information, and then put a hard copy of the list into each of your crisis response binders. Don't forget to update the list regularly.

Build a critical contacts list:

- Business contacts:
  - Alarm/Security company
  - Attorney
  - Business partner
  - Business service providers
  - Colleagues
  - Adjacent businesses
  - Pet supplies vendors
  - Property management
  - Property owner
- Financial services:
  - Accountant/CPA/Bookkeeper
  - Banker/Lender
  - Insurance agent/Broker
  - Insurance company
  - Payroll processing
  - Public insurance adjuster
- Computer services:
  - Computer hardware/Electronics vendor
  - Data backup provider

    - IT support
    - Pet care business management software vendor
    - Web designer
- Utilities providers:
    - Cellular services provider
    - Electric company
    - Gas/Propane company
    - Telephone company
    - Water company
    - Wireless provider
- Facility repairs:
    - Electrician
    - Fence repair
    - General contractor
    - HVAC repair
    - Locksmith
    - Plumber
    - Sign company
    - Snow removal
    - Tree removal
- Public services:
    - Emergency ambulance service
    - Emergency medical service

    - Fire department
    - Poison control
    - Police
    - Public works department
    - Sheriff
    - State police department
- Animal care:
    - Animal control
    - Animal shelter
    - Mutual aid contacts
    - Poison control
    - State animal response team
    - Veterinarian
- Other contacts:
    - Bottled water provider
    - Disaster remediation company
    - Dumpster rental
    - Equipment rental
    - Hiring agency for temporary workers
    - News/Media representatives
    - Vehicle rental

PART EIGHT: RESOURCES

SELECTED BIBLIOGRAPHY

ASIS International. Emergency Planning Handbook. 2nd ed., 2003.

American Veterinary Medical Association. "Disaster Preparedness for Veterinary Practices." http://www.avma.org.

________. "Emergency Preparedness and Response, April 2012." http://www.avma.org.

Baum, Neil, and John W. McDaniel. Disaster Planning for the Clinical Practice. Sudbury, MA: Jones and Bartlett Publishers, 2009.

Beren, Norris L. When Disaster Strikes Home: 101+ Ways to Protect Your Family From Unthinkable Emergencies. Mt. Prospect, IL: Emergency Preparedness Educational Institute, 2004. Kindle Edition.

Childs, Donna R. Prepare for the Worst, Plan for the Best: Disaster Preparedness and Recovery for Small Businesses. 2nd Ed. New Jersey: John Wiley and Sons, 2008.

Crow, Becky. Disaster Preparedness Guide for Small Business: You've Gotta Have a Plan! Lulu Publishing Services, 2014. Kindle Edition.

Crowther, Ethan. When Disaster Strikes: How to Deal with Worst Case Scenarios in Small Business and How to Avoid Them. 2013. Kindle Edition.

Federal Emergency Management Agency. "Are You Ready? Your Guide to Disaster Preparedness, H-34." Washington, DC: FEMA, September 1993.

________. "Emergency Management Guide for Business and Industry, FEMA-141." Washington, DC: FEMA, October 1993.

________. "National Flood Insurance Program Flood Insurance Claims Handbook, FEMA F-687." Washington, DC: FEMA, August 2014.

________. "Patterns and Findings from Current Research Citizen Preparedness Review: Community Resilience through Civic Responsibility and Self-Reliance." Business Continuity and Disaster Preparedness Planning (Issue 7: Winter 2011).

Heinke, Marsha L. "MLHCPAs 2011 Survey of Fraud, Theft and Embezzlement in Veterinary Practices." http://www.vpmp.net/.

Hoffman, Judith C. Keeping Cool on the Hot Seat: Dealing Effectively with the Media in Times of Crisis. 5th Ed. Clayton, NC: Four C's Publishing Company, 2011. Kindle Edition.

Humane Society of the United States (The). Disaster Planning for Animal Facilities. Washington, DC: HSUS. 2000.

Lee, James D., Steve Healy, and Marc Lee. The One Book You Need to Plan for Emergencies. Atlanta, GA: Whitman Publishing, LLC, 2012.

Lipman, Ira A. How to Be Safe: Protect Yourself, Your Home, Your Family, and Your Business from Crime. New York, NY: The Reader's Digest Association, Inc.: 2012.

Miller, Deborah C. Business Continuity and Disaster Recovery: Getting Started Guide: Concepts and Definitions for Common Sense Planning. 2nd ed. 2013. Kindle Edition.

Mitroff, Ian I. Why Some Companies Emerge Stronger and Better from a Crisis: 7 Essential Lessons for Surviving Disaster. New York: American Management Association, 2005. Kindle Edition.

Myers, Kenneth N. Business Continuity Strategies: Protecting Against Unplanned Disasters. 3rd Ed. New Jersey: John Wiley and Sons, 2006.

Occupational Safety and Health Administration. "How to Plan for Workplace Emergencies OSHA-3088." Washington, DC: OSHA, 2001.

_________. "Small Business Handbook OSHA 2209-02R." Washington, DC: OSHA, 2005.

Rawlings, Anthony J. How to Handle Critical Crisis: A Quick Reference Guide on How to Manage Workplace Emergencies. Atlanta, GA: LDB Entertainment, 2012. Smashwords Edition.

Schulz, Kathryn. "The Really Big One", New Yorker, July 20, 2015, http://www.newyorker.com/magazine/2015/07/20/the-really-big-one.

Seese, Michael. Scrappy Business Contingency Planning: How to Bullet-Proof Your Business and Laugh at Volcanoes, Tornadoes, Locust Plagues, and Hard Drives. Cupertino, CA: Scrappy About, 2010. Kindle Edition.

Watters, Jamie. The Business Continuity Management Desk Reference Guide to Business Continuity Planning, Crisis Management and IT Disaster Recovery. Leverage Publishing at Smashwords, 2010.

Winter, Robert. Disaster Manual for Financial Recovery: A Self Help Guide to Receive the Most Disaster Funds. Las Vegas, NV: 2015. Kindle Edition.

INTERNET AND COMMUNITY RESOURCES

All Hazards Preparedness for Rural Communities
http://www.prep4agthreats.org/

American Red Cross/Ready Rating
http://www.redcross.org
http://www.readyrating.org

Centers for Disease Control and Prevention. "Emergency Preparedness."
http://www.cdc.gov

Community Emergency Response Team (city and county level preparation)
http://www.ready.gov/citizen-corps

Department of Homeland Security
http://www.dhs.gov

Department of Labor
http://www.dol.gov/opa/flood-recovery.htm
http://workforcesecurity.doleta.gov/unemploy/disaster.asp

EDEN—Extension Disaster Education Network
http://eden.lsu.edu/Pages/default.aspx

Federal Emergency Management Agency
http://www.fema.gov
http://www.ready.gov

Groomer's Emergency Assistance Fund
http://www.geaf2013.org

Hartford Financial Services Group (The). "Disaster Planning for Businesses."
http://www.thehartford.com

Insurance Information Institute
http://www.iii.org

Insurance Institute for Business and Home Safety
Risk Identification by ZIP Code
http://www.disastersafety.org

Internal Revenue Service. "Publication 547: Casualties, Disasters, and Thefts (Business and Nonbusiness)." 2014.
http://www.irs.gov

National Flood Insurance Program
http://www.floodsmart.gov

National Oceanic and Atmospheric Administration
http://www.noaa.gov

State Animal Response Teams (Each state has a team)

US Small Business Administration
http://www.sba.gov
http://www.preparemybusiness.org

U.S. Chamber of Commerce Foundation National Disaster Help Desk for Business
https://www.uschamberfoundation.org/corporate-citizenship-center/disaster-help-desk-business

CELL PHONE APPLICATIONS

FEMA
http://www.fema.gov/mobile-app

National Weather Service
http://www.nws.noaa.gov/com/weatherreadynation/mobilephone.html

Red Cross
http://www.redcross.org/get-help/prepare-for-emergencies/mobile-apps

FOR FURTHER STUDY

http://training.fema.gov/is/
IS-10.A: Animals in Disasters: Awareness and Preparedness
IS-11.A: Animals in Disasters: Community Planning
IS-22: Are You Ready? An In-depth Guide to Citizen Preparedness
IS-106.16: Workplace Violence Awareness Training
IS-394.A: Protecting Your Home or Small Business from Disaster
IS-906: Workplace Security Awareness

Just In Case: Essentials of Disaster Preparedness for Your Veterinary Clinic
The Humane Society of the United States
http://www.youtube.com/watch?v=jm9QGDZ-L-I

EMPLOYEE EDUCATION

American Veterinary Medical Association. "Saving the Whole Family: Disaster Preparedness."
http://www.avma.org

Disaster Preparedness and Pets
AmerVetMedAssn
https://www.youtube.com/watch?v=XXVLaIlgZ2g

Disaster Preparedness for Pets
MyVNN
https://www.youtube.com/watch?v=QMEGf2Ja7uc

Get Prepared - Your 72 Hour Emergency Preparedness Plan
searchmontfire
https://www.youtube.com/watch?v=VXf2ZCzaH7k

How to Prepare to Shelter in Place
USUExtension
https://www.youtube.com/watch?v=N6b4dzwnev0

NEWS SOURCES

Amarillo Globe News, The; Amarillo, TX

Business Journals, The; Charlotte, NC

Chicago Tribune, The; Chicago, IL

Cincinnati.com (USA Today Network); Cincinnati, OH

Daily Mail; London, UK

DVM360.com; Lenexa, KS

Hamptonroads.com; Richmond, VA

Herald, The; Snohomish, WA

Hudsonreporter.com; Hudson County, NJ

Joplin Globe, The; Joplin, MO

KHNL, Hawaii News Now; Honolulu, HI

KRON, Channel 4; San Francisco, CA

KWCH Eyewitness News 12; Wichita, KS

Lawrence Journal-World; Lawrence, KS

Los Angeles Times; Los Angeles, CA

Mlive.com; Lansing, MI

New York Post, The; New York, NY

News 12 The Bronx; Bronx, NY

News 6; Orlando, FL

Newsnet 5; Cleveland, OH

Nooganomics.com; Chattanooga, TN

NT News; Darwin, NT, Australia

Pantagraph, The; Bloomington, IL

Redding Record Searchlight; Redding, CA

Seattle Times; Seattle, WA

Southern Chester County Weeklies, The; West Chester, PA

St. Louis Post-Times; St. Louis, MO

State, The; Columbia, SC

Veterinary Information Network; Davis, CA

WFMJ; Youngstown, OH

WTHR, Channel 13; Indianapolis, IN

WVIR, Channel 29; Charlottesville, VA

Valleycentral.com, Channel 4; Edinburgh, TX

APPENDIX:

CUSTOMIZABLE CRISIS RESPONSE PLAN FOR PET CARE BUSINESSES

YOUR BUSINESS NAME CRISIS RESPONSE PLAN

TABLE OF CONTENTS

YOUR BUSINESS NAME CRISIS RESPONSE PLAN

BINDER INFORMATION

Business name	
Owner's name	
Business address	
Mailing address	
Business phone	
Alternate phone	
Email	
Website	

Location of binders

Binder one of three	
Binder two of three (facility disaster kit)	
Binder three of three (offsite)	

People who have keys to the facility

Name and contact information	
Name and contact information	
Name and contact information	

YOUR BUSINESS NAME CRISIS RESPONSE PLAN

COMMUNICATION PLAN

Make notes on URLs, basic message content and frequency of notifications. Refer to pages 95-97 (Communication Plan) for details on completing this chart.

Employees

Employee contact tree	
Password-only website	

Clients

Phone (clients with animals currently at the facility)	
Public website	
Social media	

Public

Public website	
Social media	

YOUR BUSINESS NAME CRISIS RESPONSE PLAN

KEY PERSON LETTERS

Draft letters to clients, suppliers and staff that can be used if a tragedy occurs. Keep current copies filed in this section.

YOUR BUSINESS NAME CRISIS RESPONSE PLAN

EMPLOYEE CONTACT TREE

A portion of the employee contact tree is shown here as an example. A complete chart is available for download at (http://petbusinessdisasterresponse.com/crisis_plan/).

Last update: ___________________
(This list is to be considered proprietary information and is not for general distribution.)

<table>
<tr><td rowspan="6">Tier One Employee
(Owner or Manager)
Main Phone:
Alt Phone:
Email:</td><td rowspan="6">Tier Two Employee
Main Phone:
Alt Phone:
Email:</td><td rowspan="3">Tier Three Employee
Main Phone:
Alt Phone:
Email:</td><td>Tier Four Employee
Main Phone:
Alt Phone:
Email:</td></tr>
<tr><td>Tier Four Employee
Main Phone:
Alt Phone:
Email:</td></tr>
<tr><td>Tier Four Employee
Main Phone:
Alt Phone:
Email:</td></tr>
<tr><td rowspan="3">Tier Three Employee
Main Phone:
Alt Phone:
Email:</td><td>Tier Four Employee
Main Phone:
Alt Phone:
Email:</td></tr>
<tr><td>Tier Four Employee
Main Phone:
Alt Phone:
Email:</td></tr>
<tr><td>Tier Four Employee
Main Phone:
Alt Phone:
Email:</td></tr>
</table>

YOUR BUSINESS NAME CRISIS RESPONSE PLAN

EMPLOYEE SKILLS AND CROSS-TRAINING

Note which employees have CPR, bilingual, pet CPR, vet tech, computer skills, social media skills or other skills that may be helpful in a crisis. If any employee has been cross-trained, make a note of the additional training.

Employee name	Skills	Cross-trained

YOUR BUSINESS NAME CRISIS RESPONSE PLAN

CRITICAL CONTACT LIST

An example of the first page of the critical contact list is shown. A complete chart is available for download at (http://petbusinessdisasterresponse.com/crisis_plan/).

Last update: ___________________

(This list is to be considered proprietary information and is not for general distribution.)

	Contact	Contact Name	Phone Number	Alternate Phone	Physical Address	Email
BUSINESS CONTACTS	Alarm/Security company					
	Attorney					
	Business partner					
	Business service providers					
	Colleagues					
	Adjacent businesses					
	Pet supplies vendors					
	Property management					
	Property owner					

YOUR BUSINESS NAME CRISIS RESPONSE PLAN

BUILDING MAP

The building map that you include here can be simply hand-drawn on graph paper or it can be of architectural quality. Your goal is to be able to communicate accurate information to first responders as quickly as possible.

Your building map should show as much detail as possible including, but not limited to:

- Alarm control
- Designated escape routes
- Exits
- Fire extinguishers
- Fire suppression systems
- Floor plans
- High-value items
- Restricted areas
- Stairways
- Utility shutoffs

YOUR BUSINESS NAME CRISIS RESPONSE PLAN

HAZARDOUS MATERIALS

Include copies of safety data sheets if you have them available. Make a note if there is any chemical on your property that could pose a hazard to first responders or to the environment.

Cleaning supplies are located

Paint and other chemicals are located

Other hazardous materials (note type and specific location)

YOUR BUSINESS NAME CRISIS RESPONSE PLAN

SITE MAP

A site map shows the entire property (buildings and grounds) and should indicate any other relevant information:

- Electrical cutoffs
- Fencing/Gates
- Fire hydrants (if close to the property)
- Gas lines
- Gas main valves
- Hazardous materials (including cleaning supplies and chemicals)
- High-value items
- Location of each building
- Propane tanks
- Restricted areas
- Sewer lines
- Storm drains
- Water lines
- Water main valves

YOUR BUSINESS NAME CRISIS RESPONSE PLAN

AREA MAP

- Include a current street map of the area so that you can direct employees and customers to you in case of street closures.
- Mark several routes
- Post this information to your website and social media sites
- Email map to employees and clients if possible

YOUR BUSINESS NAME CRISIS RESPONSE PLAN

LOCALIZED EVACUATION CHECKLIST

Adjust this list to fit your facility's needs. Add details as necessary. Include alternates across shifts for each assignment.

Action	Assigned to (individual or team)
Call 911 if alarm system has not automatically sent notification	
Immediately release any employee whose health could be negatively affected by the crisis	
Evacuate animals on leads or in Evacsacks and crate them once they are safely outside of the building	
Move animals to a predetermined evacuation location	
Unplug equipment if time permits	
Close all windows and doors (especially fire-rated doors) if time permits	
Shut off electrical breakers, gas and water (but do not turn back on until given clearance)	
What to grab: Disaster binder Facility disaster kit Identification Keys Date book/appointment calendar Cell phone and charger Laptop or tablet and power cords Current controlled drug log	

YOUR BUSINESS NAME CRISIS RESPONSE PLAN

LOCALIZED EVACUATION CHECKLIST

Action	Assigned to (individual or team)
Move vehicles to a predetermined safe location	
Leave someone outside of your facility to communicate with first responders	
Perform a head count of employees	
Perform a head count of animals	
Contact clients with your evacuation location and pickup procedures	
Release remaining off-shift employees after all of the animals that have not been picked up have been moved to an alternate location	
On-shift employees should report to the alternate location	

YOUR BUSINESS NAME CRISIS RESPONSE PLAN

COMMUNITY-WIDE EVACUATION CHECKLIST

Adjust this list to fit your facility's needs. Add details as necessary. Include alternates across shifts for each assignment.

Action	Assigned to (individual or team)
Listen to radio or television newscasts and follow the instructions given by the authorities	
Load disaster kit into main vehicle in case evacuation notice is given	
Contact pet owners and have as many pets collected as possible	
Bring loose objects into the facility to prevent them becoming hazardous in unstable weather conditions	
Pre-assemble travel crates	
Make sure that each vehicle that will be used in the evacuation is fueled and has an evacuation map	
Load pets (in travel crates) into vehicles	
Check every area for hiders and keep a written head count as each animal is loaded	
Release employees who have home commitments	

YOUR BUSINESS NAME CRISIS RESPONSE PLAN

COMMUNITY-WIDE EVACUATION CHECKLIST

Action	Assigned to (individual or team)
What to grab: Disaster binder Identification Keys Date book/appointment calendar Cell phone and charger Laptop or tablet and power cords Current controlled drug log	
Unplug equipment	
Close all windows and doors (especially fire-rated doors)	
Shut off electrical breakers, gas and water	
Secure premises	
Decide which evacuation route to take	
Post sign on door informing clients that you have evacuated. Provide contact information for new location along with your cell number	
Release employees who will not be going to your evacuation destination	
Contact alarm company	
Contact evacuation location to let them know you are on your way	
Contact all employees regularly to give status updates	
Keep in contact with clients	

YOUR BUSINESS NAME CRISIS RESPONSE PLAN

COMMUNITY-WIDE EVACUATION MAP

Mark two or more routes on the same map.

Destinations should be at least 100 miles away from your current location.

Communicate your location to the public via your website and through social media.

Leave a copy of the map on the front door of your facility. Keep clients and employees up to date regarding your estimated return date.

YOUR BUSINESS NAME CRISIS RESPONSE PLAN

CONTACT INFORMATION FOR COMMUNITY-WIDE EVACUATION

Make contacts now. Check yearly to confirm accurate information.

Have alternate accommodations for each destination. Include a veterinary clinic contact for each location.

Contact information for person who will always know my whereabouts	
First destination	
Alternate accommodations	
Vetcrinary contact	
Other information	
Second destination	
Alternate accommodations	
Veterinary contact	
Other information	

YOUR BUSINESS NAME CRISIS RESPONSE PLAN

MUTUAL AID AGREEMENTS

Set up mutual aid agreements while you are writing your plan:

- Mutual aid agreements do not have to be made with other pet facilities; any appropriate business that is willing to accommodate your animals is acceptable.
- Make agreements with businesses both locally and at each of your evacuation destinations.
- Outline the nature of the agreements in simple form (no more than one page).
- You may need to agree to pay for space.
- Make alternate arrangements for each location.
- Add contact information for each location to your critical contact list.

YOUR BUSINESS NAME CRISIS RESPONSE PLAN

SHELTER-IN-PLACE CHECKLIST

Adjust this list to fit your facility's needs. Add details as necessary. Include alternates across shifts for each assignment.

Action	Assigned to (individual or team)
Keep track of the situation with a NOAA weather radio and listen to regular TV or radio bands to hear the latest instructions for your area	
Pre-assemble travel crates and move them into your safe room	
Move facility disaster kit to your safe room	
Close the business and ask all clients and visitors to stay	
Close and lock all windows and exterior doors	
Turn off all vents, air-conditioning units and fans	
Turn off air exchangers and air filters	
What to grab: Disaster binder Identification Keys Date book/appointment calendar Cell phone and charger Laptop or tablet and power cords Current controlled drug log	

YOUR BUSINESS NAME CRISIS RESPONSE PLAN

SHELTER-IN-PLACE CHECKLIST

Action	Assigned to (individual or team)
Bring all animals into the safe area and put them into travel crates after checking for animals that may be hiding	
Close and lock the door to the safe room	
Seal off windows, doors and vents if there is a chance of contamination	
Ask employees and others in the safe room to call their emergency contacts to let them know where they are and that they are safe	
Change the message on your answering machine or messaging service to state your shelter-in-place status	
Write down the names of all of the people and animals in the safe room and secure this list by taping it to the wall	
Contact clients with your shelter-in-place information	
Contact employees who are scheduled for shifts and advise them of your shelter-in-place status	
Keep listening to the radio or television until you are told by authorities that it is safe to leave your shelter	
Keep in touch with clients throughout the shelter-in-place period	

YOUR BUSINESS NAME CRISIS RESPONSE PLAN

RETURN AND RECOVERY CHECKLIST

Detail in advance how designated staff will return to your facility after an emergency to assess conditions, document damage, and determine when it is safe to welcome back remaining employees and customers.

Action	Assigned to (individual or team)
Use the employee contact tree to get in touch with employees	
Check on-site animals and staff for injuries	
Initiate client communication plan	
Notify outside agencies of status if necessary	
Make calls to critical contact list as necessary (notify authorities if controlled drug box has been damaged or is missing)	
Contact insurance companies	
Assess and document damage to facility, supplies, inventory and equipment	
Take photos before cleanup or repair	
Clean and disinfect what you plan to reuse	
Have utilities turned on after all systems are checked by professionals	

YOUR BUSINESS NAME CRISIS RESPONSE PLAN

RETURN AND RECOVERY CHECKLIST

Action	Assigned to (individual or team)
Inspect and test all electronics at least twice	
File insurance reports	
Schedule cleanup and repair	
Communicate reopening plans with clients and the public	
Restock facility first aid kit and facility disaster kit	
Review crisis plan and response with staff members and modify the plan if necessary	

YOUR BUSINESS NAME CRISIS RESPONSE PLAN

EMERGENCY POLICIES AND PROCEDURES

In this section, you will answer questions that are specific to your business policies. Consult state and federal laws regarding overtime employment and other subjects before putting these guidelines into play.

Some issues that you might want to address in this section include:

- Absentee/Overtime policy
- Employees' animals
- Extra expenses
- Facility and employee security policies
- How will we charge for services and materials? (Normal rates, disaster rates or materials-only are some alternatives)
- If we are able to accept animals, will we take only current clients' animals?
- Pet pickup policies for alternate location and community-wide evacuation
- Media and social media guidelines
- Stray animal policy
- Vaccination policy
- Who is authorized to make decisions in your absence?
- Who is authorized to make decisions regarding evacuation?

YOUR BUSINESS NAME CRISIS RESPONSE PLAN

BANK AND FINANCIAL INFORMATION

Complete this form for each bank with which you do business. Adapt the form to your needs.

Also include in this section:

- A color copy of each signatory's driver's license and social security card
- Copies (front and back) of each business credit card
- A pencil case containing a supply of cash (in small bills) and blank business checks

Company name	
Branch address	
Branch phone number	
Customer service phone number	
Bank website	
Bank account number	
Savings account number	
Money market account number	
Authorized signatories on accounts	

YOUR BUSINESS NAME CRISIS RESPONSE PLAN

INSURANCE INFORMATION AND POLICY COPIES

Continue with workers' compensation insurance, disability insurance, auto insurance and any other business insurance policies that you have in force.

A complete copy of each policy should be included in this section.

Business insurance company	
Address	
Customer service phone number	
Agent's name	
Agent's phone number	
Policy number	
Life insurance company	
Address	
Customer service phone number	
Agent's name	
Agent's phone number	
Policy number	
Health insurance company	
Address	
Customer service phone number	
Agent's name	
Agent's phone number	
Policy number	

YOUR BUSINESS NAME CRISIS RESPONSE PLAN

COPY OF FACILITY LEASE OR MORTGAGE INFORMATION

Copies of all relevant lease or mortgage documents, including extensions and addendums, go into this section. Make sure that payment information is included in the copy or include it on this page.

YOUR BUSINESS NAME CRISIS RESPONSE PLAN

WRITTEN INVENTORY OF FACILITY FURNITURE, FIXTURES AND EQUIPMENT

Inventory last completed (sign and date this line): ________________________________

- List items room by room
- Include serial numbers and model numbers for all electrical equipment
- Add specific information; details will mean a lot when you're trying to get the insurance company to settle a claim in your favor
- CDs with photos of the facility should be placed in this section

Your business property insurance policy should be written to reimburse you for replacement value; include receipts if you can locate them. Otherwise, keep copies of receipts going forward.

YOUR BUSINESS NAME CRISIS RESPONSE PLAN

COPIES OF SOFTWARE LICENSES AND INSTALLATION DISKS

List serial and registration numbers here.

Add copies of contracts or written agreements with software providers and IT providers.

Copies of warranties could also be included in this section.

YOUR BUSINESS NAME CRISIS RESPONSE PLAN

IMPORTANT PASSWORDS AND PINS

Include the passwords that you may need in the event of an emergency: bank, credit card, debit card, professional associations, etc. Update this page each time you change a PIN or password.

NOTE: If you can, use a generic name for each account, so that if this list is accessed by someone unauthorized, they will have a harder time accessing your accounts.

Account	Log-in	Password or PIN

YOUR BUSINESS NAME CRISIS RESPONSE PLAN

HARD COPIES OF BUSINESS-RELATED FORMS

These forms may be stored in "the cloud," but you could find yourself without a printer, or even a computer to access the files.

- Any form to which you may need instant access:
- Registration form
- Boarding form
- Blank invoice
- Policies and procedures
- Employee manual

List the included forms on this page. When a document is updated, all of your binders should receive the new revision.

YOUR BUSINESS NAME CRISIS RESPONSE PLAN

CLIENTS' EMERGENCY INFORMATION AND VETERINARY RELEASE

Emergency cards are essential to your communication plan. Clients should complete a card when registering their animal for your services for the first time. Explain to your clients that this is part of your emergency plan.

An emergency contact and veterinary release file is included on the *Hairy Situations* website (http://petbusinessdisasterresponse.com/crisis_plan/) in Word format. I suggest that you have these cards printed on card stock in 3×5-inch or 5×7-inch format and punch holes in the cards so that they can be held together with ring binders. If you include index card dividers, you can find any card in a hurry.

This information is meant to be used when the disaster binder is brought into use. You will want to keep the hard copies with the disaster binder that is included in your facility disaster kit. You may also want to have this information in electronic form on the flash drive in each of your binders for ease of general notification.

The owner's signature on the card will allow you to seek alternate care in an emergency.

File the cards by the dog's first name; this will simplify the process of specific notification in case an employee is not familiar with the owner's last name.

Emergency contact should NOT be a spouse, close relative or other person that may be affected by the same crisis event.

YOUR BUSINESS NAME CRISIS RESPONSE PLAN

CLIENTS' EMERGENCY INFORMATION AND VETERINARY RELEASE

EMERGENCY INFORMATION/VETERINARY RELEASE	
Please print clearly	
Pet's name:	Microchip #:
Owner's full name:	
Owner's email address:	
1st contact number:	
2nd contact number:	
Name and contact information of the person who will pick up my pet if I cannot be contacted:	
YOUR BUSINESS NAME has my permission to seek care for my pet in the event of a building evacuation or community-wide disaster. I understand that attempts will be made to contact me before such care is sought. This agreement covers veterinary care, shelter care or other related care that YOUR BUSINESS NAME deems appropriate for my pet. I understand that I will be responsible for all costs related to the care of my pet during an emergency situation.	
Pet owner's signature:	Date:

YOUR BUSINESS NAME CRISIS RESPONSE PLAN

BINDER UPDATE RECORD

Add tasks to this list that are meaningful for your business.

Task	Date of completion (date and initials)									
New equipment/furnishings added to inventory										
CDs updated to reflect new equipment/ furnishings										
Recharge fire extinguishers										
Telephone tree checked/ updated										
Critical contacts list checked/updated										
Maps checked/updated										
Financial information checked/updated										
New insurance policies added to binder										
Disaster supplies rotated										
Employee training in fire extinguisher and disaster kit										
Plan tested										

ABOUT THE AUTHOR

Sonya Wilson began working with dogs at a very early age, standing with her four-legged siblings at the fence and barking at sanitation workers. The strategy was successful; and she has lived with dogs ever since.

A descendant of early Texas settlers, Sonya earned a Bachelor of Science degree in Elementary Education from Texas A&M University and holds a lifetime teaching certificate.

Ms. Wilson has been training dogs since 1990. In 2002, she opened Austin, Texas' first completely kennel free canine daycare, Southpaws Playschool. Sonya trains pet professionals and pet owners in pet first aid and emergency preparation and response through Four Legged First Aid, a program she originated in 2011.

Sonya spends most of her time working with the dogs at Southpaws Playschool (including her own six random-bred dogs). Sonya's goal as a canine day care owner and trainer is to make a positive, loving impact on the dogs in her care.

Author photo by Steve Armstrong Photography

Made in the USA
Columbia, SC
06 October 2021